D0966915

Twayne's United States Authors Series

EDITOR OF THIS VOLUME

Warren French

Robert Anderson

TUSAS 300

Photo Credit: Peter Fink

Robert Anderson

ROBERT ANDERSON

By THOMAS P. ADLER
Purdue University

TWAYNE PUBLISHERS
A DIVISION OF G. K. HALL & CO., BOSTON

First Printing

Library of Congress Cataloging in Publication Data

Adler, Thomas P.
Robert Anderson.

(Twayne's United States authors series ; 300)
Bibliography: p. 177–80
Includes index.
1. Anderson, Robert Woodruff, 1917–
Criticism and interpretation.
PS3501.N34Z56 812'.5'4 77-15103
ISBN 0-8057-7204-9

MANUFACTURED IN THE UNITED STATES OF AMERICA

For Winnie

Contents

About the Author
Acknowledgments
Chronology
Preface
1. Introduction: Life and Art 15
2. The "Learning Plays" 28
3. The Maturation Plays 54
4. Writing for Film 86
5. The Marriage Plays 102
6. "Plays for Saturday" — And One for Monday 123
7. The Theme is Loneliness 145
8. Conclusion 163
Notes and References 167
Selected Bibliography 177
Index 181

About the Author

Thomas P. Adler received his A.B. and A.M. degrees from Boston College, and his Ph.D. from the University of Illinois at Urbana. Since 1970, he has taught courses in medieval, Elizabethan, and modern drama, as well as in film history and aesthetics, at Purdue University, where he is currently Associate Professor of English. He has published widely in the field of modern drama, with articles on O'Neill, Williams, Albee, Arden, and Pinter, among others, appearing in such journals as *Arizona Quarterly, Renascence, Educational Theatre Journal, Modern Drama,* and *The Quarterly Journal of Speech.* Two of his essays on Tennessee Williams are reprinted in the Twentieth Century Views collection; he has completed a critical study of the Pulitzer Prize Plays, and is now at work on a book on language in the plays of Edward Albee.

Preface

For the past quarter century, since 1953 when *Tea and Sympathy* opened on Broadway, the name Robert Anderson has meant literate, well-crafted, highly sensitive plays about loneliness and disillusionment, marriage and middle age. While he cannot claim a place among the major theatrical figures of this century, his plays have been generally well received by the critics and popular with audiences not only in this country but around the world. Four of his dramas have been chosen for inclusion in the Best American Plays or Best Plays series or both. Two of his filmscripts have won Academy Award nominations. And over two dozen countries have staged productions of his works.

Yet despite such worldwide exposure and familiarity, there has been, with the exception of brief reviews, virtually no critical attention to Anderson's writing, although it has become the subject of college seminars and doctoral dissertations. This book is therefore intended to fill that void by serving as an introduction to what is by now a substantial body of work. I limit my discussion — with the exception of one unproduced, original screenplay that Mr. Anderson thought it particularly valuable to consider — to those works that have been either produced or published: ten plays, five filmscripts, and a novel. Along with analyzing the structure, characterization, symbolism, language, themes, and, where appropriate, stagecraft of each of these works, I also attempt to place the playwright within the development of modern (especially American) drama, hoping to arrive at a balanced assessment of his strengths and weaknesses and of his original contribution to the contemporary theater.

Because the autobiographical impetus is more than normally operative in Anderson's writing, the first chapter deals at some length with the relevant facts of his life and then attempts to present in systematic fashion his ideas on playwriting and the theater developed throughout a career as teacher-dramatist that now spans three decades. Thereafter, since Anderson reworks, modifies, and refines the same situations, themes, and character configurations in his plays, a chronological approach will best chart his maturation as a playwright. Thus Chapters 2 and 3, and 5, 6, and 7 each explicate in order of composition two or three of his major works, while Chapter 4 analyzes Anderson's work as a screenwriter, particularly in the late fifties and early sixties. The concluding, evaluative chapter provides an overview and synthesis of the patterns and motifs that emerge throughout Anderson's writing, suggesting finally that implicit in it is a criticism of the American tendency to dichotomize reason and emotion and to stereotype male and female roles so that open expression of feeling comes to be regarded as somehow unmanly, with the result that Anderson's protagonists often overcompensate for this forced denial of feeling by clinging to an adolescent, idealized notion of sexuality.

In undertaking this study, I was assisted, in ways both large and small, by many people to whom I owe my gratitude. Ms. Audrey Wood, Anderson's literary agent; Allen Rivkin of the Writers Guild of America, West; and Ms. Maria Reichardt of the Historical Sound Recordings Department at the Yale University Library all answered my queries promptly. Henry F. Bedford, librarian at Phillips Exeter Academy; Ms. Camille Croce of The Dramatists Guild; Nigel D.J. Duncan of the Edinburgh (Scotland) *Evening News;* and Ms. Lois Hamby and James M. Roberts of the Academy of Motion Picture Arts and Sciences all supplied me with material either by or about Mr. Anderson. In that regard, I am particularly indebted to David H. Ayers, executive director of the American Playwrights Theater, who furnished me with tapes of two interviews with Mr. Anderson. And the staffs of the New York Public Library of the Performing Arts at Lincoln Center and of the Interlibrary Loan Division at the Purdue University Library greatly facilitated my research, as did the Purdue Research Foundation through the award of a Summer Faculty XL Grant.

Robert Anderson has graciously supplied me with unpublished manuscripts, submitted to a taped interview, and corresponded with me regularly for over a year. Though he knew that he would not agree with all my conclusions, and though he preferred not to read this manuscript (which is in no sense an authorized study), he was as kind and as genuinely interested in my work as his plays had led me to believe he would be. My greatest debt is to my family and friends: to my colleague, A.A. DeVitis, for his careful reading of the text; to my sons, Jeremy and Christopher, too young to know what scholarly research and writing are, yet old enough to realize that I was upstairs working when I might have been spending more time with them. And especially to my wife, Winnie — to whom this book is dedicated — for her help in proofreading and preparing the index, but mostly for her quiet, patient support.

It is necessary to insert one note on a peculiarity of Mr. Anderson's punctuation. Oftentimes, instead of using a period, he will use ellipsis marks (. . .) even when nothing has been omitted. Consequently, in quotations from his writings, three dots simply reproduce Anderson's own notation, whereas four dots indicate that I have omitted a portion of the passage.

THOMAS P. ADLER

West Lafayette, Indiana

Acknowledgments

Quotations from Robert Anderson's copyrighted works *After, I Never Sang for My Father, Silent Night, Lonely Night, Solitaire/Double Solitaire, Tea and Sympathy,* and *You Know I Can't Hear You When the Water's Running* appear by the permission of the publisher, Random House, Inc.

Quotations from *All Summer Long,* Copyright© 1955 by Robert Anderson, reprinted by permission of Samuel French, Inc.

Quotations from *The Days Between* appear with the permission of Ms. Bridget Aschenberg of International Creative Management.

Quotations from *A Wreath and a Curse* by Donald Wetzel, Copyright© 1950 by Donald Wetzel, used by permission of Crown Publishers, Inc.

Quotations from "Robert Anderson: Playwright of Middle-Aged Loneliness," by Thomas P. Adler, appear by permission of the editors of the *Ball State University Forum,* where the article appeared in Spring 1975 (XVI, ii: 58–64).

Chronology

(Unless otherwise indicated, works cited are plays and dates are of the first production.)

1917 Born April 28 in New York City, second son of James H. and Myra Grigg Anderson.

1931-1935 Attended Phillips Exeter Academy.

1935-1942 Attended Harvard University. A.B. *(magna cum laude),* 1939; M.A., 1940.

1940 Married to Phyllis Stohl.

1942-1946 Served as a lieutenant in the United States Navy; awarded the Bronze Star.

1945 *Come Marching Home* wins National Theater Conference Prize.

1946 Awarded a Rockefeller fellowship.

1946-1950 Taught playwriting at the American Wing Theater.

1948 *The Eden Rose.*

1948-1953 Wrote adaptations for the Theater Guild of the Air.

1951 *Love Revisited.*

1953 *All Summer Long; Tea and Sympathy.* Elected to membership in The Playwrights Company.

1955-1956 Taught playwriting at The Actors Studio.

1956 Film version of *Tea and Sympathy.* Phyllis Stohl Anderson dies.

1957 *Until They Sail* (filmscript).

1959 *Silent Night, Lonely Night; The Nun's Story* (filmscript). Married to Teresa Wright.

1959-1960 President of the New Dramatists Committee.

1962 *A Small Part of a Long Story* (unproduced filmscript).

1965 *The Days Between* produced by the American Playwrights Theater.

1966 *The Sand Pebbles* (filmscript).

1967 *You Know I Can't Hear You When the Water's Running.*

1968 *I Never Sang for My Father.* On the faculty of the Salzburg Seminar in American Studies.

1970 Film version of *I Never Sang for My Father*. Presented with the Writers Guild of America Award.

1971 *Solitaire/Double Solitaire.*

1971-1973 President of The Dramatists Guild.

1973 *After* (novel).

CHAPTER 1

Introduction: Life and Art

AT the beginning of Robert Anderson's most autobiographical play, *I Never Sang for My Father* (1968), the narrator and central character Gene Garrison — like the dramatist himself, a writer-teacher who has suffered the loss through death of his wife and father — muses to the audience: "Death ends a life but it does not end a relationship, which struggles on in the survivor's mind toward some final resolution, some clear meaning, which it perhaps never finds."[1] At the end of the play, Gene haltingly and with less assurance repeats virtually these same words, modified slightly yet significantly: he now omits the word "perhaps," and so it is a resolution and meaning that experience has told him the mind "never finds."[2] In this, Gene is clearly the playwright's alter ego, for Anderson himself, speaking about "the closest relationships" of his personal life, has said: "I relive these relationships over and over again," wondering "couldn't it have been different."[3] And he relives them not only in his mind, but in his dramas, filmscripts, and fiction as well, where he has limned his own psychobiography.

I *Education and Early Development*

Anderson's earliest ventures into writing for the theater — a one act play adapted from "a now forgotten opera libretto"[4] while a student at Exeter, and an adaptation of LeCoq's comic operetta *Girofle-Girofla* as well as the librettos, music, and lyrics for two of the Dunster House Christmas shows, including one named *Hour Town,* at Harvard — not only reflected his long-standing love for music but presaged his lengthy career in playwriting as well. Born in New York City on April 28, 1917, Anderson had intended throughout his boyhood and adolescence to become an opera singer; a progressively worsening sinus condition, however, forced a curtailment of these plans and, by midway in his undergraduate days, his decision to write his own plays rather than appear in the works of others was crystalizing.

Emotionally and temperamentally, the young Anderson always felt closer to his mother than to his father. James H. Anderson, who once ran for mayor of New Rochelle, where the family lived while sons Donald (now a physician) and Robert were growing up, seemed to embody the American rags-to-riches story, as Tom Garrison does in *I Never Sang for My Father.* Although he experienced a temporary reversal and lost his executive position with the United Verde Copper Company in the 1929 crash, by the time his sons were enrolled at Harvard he had once again become financially successful, this time in the insurance business. If the self-made and self-reliant James was responsible for instilling in his sons their interest in athletics (Anderson still enjoys playing tennis), it was their mother, the former Myra Grigg, who imbued Robert with his avocation for gardening and his love of the arts, especially music and the theater; the fond portraits of the mothers in several works, particularly Nan Hilton in *The Eden Rose* (1948) and Margaret Garrison in *I Never Sang for My Father* form his homage to her. The cultural and emotional gulf between Anderson's parents created in the home a microcosm of the archetypal conflict between the materialistic and the artistic sensibility — making the family's problems similar, if in a less aggravated form, to the ones O'Neill dramatizes in *A Long Day's Journey Into Night* — and provided Anderson's work with one of its recurring motifs.

After attending a progressive private grammar school in New Rochelle and spending one summer at art school, Anderson enrolled for prep school at Phillips Exeter Academy in Exeter, New Hampshire, supported partially by scholarship aid and working as a waiter and later by serving as a dormitory proctor. He countered the inevitable loneliness of adolescence by participating in sports (basketball, track, and tennis) and student government, singing in the glee club, and acting in school plays. In 1935, he entered Harvard University, graduating *magna cum laude* and as class poet four years later, after having written a senior honors thesis on *The Necessity for Poetic Drama.* The thesis was largely an expression of admiration for Maxwell Anderson (no relation), who had inspired young Robert by being "one of the leaders of that stunning generation of playwrights who were making our drama the most exciting in the world."[5] Despite his valuation of poetic drama, Anderson's taste in theater at the time was eclectic, running more in the direction of comedy of manners; along with Maxwell Anderson, the American playwrights he regarded most highly were Philip Barry, S. N. Behrman, and Robert Sherwood, and, from across the Atlantic, James M. Barrie, Noel Coward, and John Van Druten.

Although Harvard at that time no longer offered any playwriting course such as George Pierce Baker's famous English 47 (to which the young O'Neill had gravitated twenty years earlier), Anderson did work under Robert Hillyer, a Pulitzer Prize winning poet. Besides writing plays, Anderson provided theater reviews for the *Harvard Advocate.* While continuing his studies in the graduate program at Harvard from 1939–1942, the industrious Anderson served as a teaching assistant in the English department there; taught literature, playwriting, and history of the theater at several small women's colleges in the Boston area; and wrote reviews for *The Atlantic* to supplement his income. He completed all his course work for the doctorate and, the day before he entered the Navy, passed his Ph.D. preliminary examination; if he had returned to finish his doctoral degree after the war, his dissertation would have been written on Tom Robertson, the nineteenth century British author of well-made "cup and saucer" dramas like *Society* and *Caste.*

During his seven years at Harvard, Anderson wrote approximately twenty one act and four full length dramas.[6] From his undergraduate days, only four one act and one long play survive. *Dream Dust,* the first of these and winner of an honorable mention in a contest sponsored by the Berkeley Playmakers, tells of a young poet befriended by a crippled old lady. It is one of the few works in which Anderson deals extensively with the illusion-reality dichotomy, a theme that recurs with prominence only once again, in the *I'm Herbert* sketch from *You Know I Can't Hear You When the Water's Running* (1967). Two others, *Death Do Us Part* and *The Gate,* mark rare excursions into a terrain uncharacteristic of Anderson — violence; the former centers on a young man who kills an older woman's husband at her instigation, while the latter, written in verse which shows the influence of Auden, Isherwood, and Spender,[7] deals with a murderer and potential suicide's need to admit his guilt. *Midnight Dialogue,* the fourth of the extant one act plays, demonstrates the influence of Coward as it recounts the story of a husband and wife acting team on tour in *Camille.* The only surviving full length play from Anderson's undergraduate days is the historical verse drama *Anthony Babington,* based on Stefan Zweig's account of the Walsingham plot but clearly modeled after the plays of Maxwell Anderson; in its focus on one who refuses to compromise his principles, it perhaps foreshadows Anderson's later treatment of John Bosworth in *Come Marching Home* (1945), while introducing a concern that recurs again and again in the playwright's work.

From his graduate school days, three full length dramas survive. The first, *Straw in the Wind* (1939), treats, within a comedy of manners framework indebted to Coward and Barry, an autobiographical subject Anderson will frequently explore later on, most notably in *All Summer Long* (1953): the unsalutary effect that a marriage short on open display of love and affection has on the children. The second, *Undiscovered Country* (1940) — a fantasy in the style of Barry's later plays — employs the Orpheus and Eurydice myth in what turned out to be for Anderson a prophetic tale of the death of a young playwright's wife. The third, and apparently the least successful, was a melodramatic and melancholy work entitled *The Sisters* (1941).

II *Life with Phyllis*

Anderson dedicated the published version of *Tea and Sympathy* (1953), his first Broadway success, to his first wife, the former Phyllis Stohl, "whose spirit is everywhere in this play and in my life."[8] Phyllis's spirit was pervasive not only in *Tea and Sympathy,* still regarded by many as his most important and enduring drama, but in everything else that Anderson would write. Though they had no children, they nurtured each other's careers; and after her death from cancer in November 1956, the loss of the wife recurs as a subject regularly, first in the background when "the ghosts of grief" (as Anderson has called them) are too close to face, then gradually emerges as a dominant motif, until, in his most recently published work, the novel *After* (1973), the author comes as close to a final resolution of the relationship that struggled on in his mind for over fifteen years as he seems likely ever to reach.

Anderson met Phyllis — who at twenty-nine was ten years older than he — during his sophomore year at Harvard, when he acted and sang in several plays she directed at the Erskine School, where she headed the theater department, while also overseeing drama at Radcliffe College. They married in June 1940. Phyllis, who held an M.F.A. degree from Yale, later became a radio scriptwriter, and then head of the play reading department and an associate producer with the Theater Guild; at the time of her death, she was a literary agent, counting among her many authors dramatists like William Inge and Paddy Chayefsky, who paid tribute, respectively, to her "simple and beautiful faith in people" and her "dignity, kindness, loyalty, steadfastness and goodness of heart" that helped others "maintain [their] belief in the essential decency of life."[9] John Wharton attests to her being "a remarkable person in many ways. She was a play agent who delighted in working with young, unestablished playwrights. In that field she was superior to anyone else.... She was not only a skillful agent; she radiated humanity. Her clients adored her. So did Bob."[10]

Separated from the woman he "adored" by his duties as a naval intelligence officer, Anderson wrote his first full length play to be seen in New York — albeit for a limited run off-Broadway — while serving as ship's secretary on the *Alaska.* Called *Come Marching Home,* it won the National Theater Conference Prize in 1944 for the best play written by a serviceman overseas, and together with two other plays penned on board ship in the sweltering heat of the Leyte Gulf in the Pacific, helped secure him a $2,000 NTC–Rockefeller fellowship in playwriting. Of those two works, one called *The Tailored Heart* has since been "mercifully lost,"[11] while the other, *Boy Grown Tall,* was obviously autobiographical in its impetus and would seem to contain the seeds for *The Days Between* (1965). In it, an idealistic and romantic young playwright — married to a director — faces the conflict between the duty to his art and the duty to his marriage, with his traditional notion of the proper roles of husband and wife thrown askew by his wife's working to support him. Anderson regards the writing scholarship, which enabled him to study under John Gassner at the dramatic workshop of the New School of Social Research upon his discharge from the Navy, as crucial in his decision to leave behind the academic life for a practicing life in the theater: "This really determined my life in a way, since the obvious move for me [would have been] to go back to Harvard to finish up with my Ph.D."[12]

Not that he gave up teaching altogether, for in the spring of 1946 he inaugurated a playwriting course for veterans at The American Theater Wing, where he taught until 1950; during 1955–1956, as an established dramatist, he would offer a similar course at The Actors Studio. In the early 1950s, he helped found the New Dramatists Committee, initially funded by The Playwrights Company as a memorial to their deceased member, Sidney Howard, and designed, Anderson says, as a "kind of workshop or rallying point for young playwrights" where they could "hear their plays read aloud by actors" and hear the craft of drama discussed by such authors as Howard Lindsay, Maxwell Anderson, Moss Hart, S. N. Behrman, and Robert Sherwood; later, when Anderson served as the organization's president (1959–1960), "There [were] still craft discussions led by people like Arthur Miller, Tennessee Williams, Harold Clurman, Lillian Hellman, Jo Mielziner, John Gassner, and Abe Burrows."[13]

While teaching others, Anderson put into practice what he himself was also learning, concentrating much of his effort during the five years between 1948 and 1953 on extensive writing for radio and television. For the Theater Guild of the Air, he "adapted thirty-six plays"[14] and several novels "to the requirements of radio, usually replete with outstanding casts,"[15] including *Valley Forge, The Petrified Forest, Dream Girl, Summer and Smoke, David Copperfield, Arrowsmith, A Farewell to Arms,* and *Of Mice and Men.*[16] And for such television programs as Studio One, Starlight Theater, and Cavalcade of America, he did no fewer than twenty-five scripts, the majority of them adaptations. Even today, he does not condescend to his work in radio and television, calling it "a terrific training ground for a young playwright";[17] "You learned economy. . . . it was doing them that made a professional writer of me."[18]

Nor did this prevent his working on original scripts. Soon after his release from the navy he began writing *The Eden Rose,* destined to become his second long play to be given a brief production, and in the same year (1946) he also wrote an inconsequential and highly unsatisfactory play called *Sublet,* as well as collaborated with the English actress Leonora Corbett on an unproduced play, *Comfort Me with Apples.* During 1947, he tried his hand at fiction — a form he would return to twenty-five years later with greater success — writing three short stories and a first novel, none of which was ever published. After composing an early draft (1948) of *Tea and Sympathy,* Anderson ventured, for the last time, into the realm of comedy of manners in *Lover, Come Back to Me,* finished in 1950 and retitled *Love Revisited* for its production the following year, when he was also engaged in the task of adapting Donald Wetzel's novel *A Wreath and a Curse* for the stage. About this lengthy apprenticeship period of prodigious activity, Anderson has commented warmly and enthusiastically: "It was a heady time. Writing plays in the mornings, radio, then later TV scripts in the afternoons, teaching three or four nights a week."[19]

But the happiness of attaining critical and popular acclaim with *Tea and Sympathy,* and artistic if not commercial success with *All Summer Long,* which had overjoyed the wife who had encouraged him so lovingly, were to be short-lived. Ironically, on the day *Love Revisited* had gone into rehearsal in 1951, Phyllis underwent her first operation for cancer, and from 1954 to her death in 1956, Robert spent most of his time caring for her. He would say, years later, "Her death, when I was in my thirties, was the greatest emotional crisis of my life."[20] It was also an artistic watershed.

III *Beginning Again*

In his essay, "No Final Curtain on the Ghosts of Grief," Anderson writes frankly and movingly — and without self-pity or rancor — of the time leading up to and following his first wife's death: "The immediate days and weeks after her death were a time of confusing opposites. A deep sense of loss, of being burned out, but also a sense of relief (which brought its own guilty feelings).... The survivor, I think, needs this combination of being able to be a normal, needful man and a bereaved husband."[21] Although in talking about this period he remembers it as a time in which he "wrote nothing of significance for six years,"[22] that is an exaggeration, since the actual time away from creative activity was not as long as it must have seemed to him; but it is true that he did not write another original play that achieved a Broadway production until *Silent Night, Lonely Night* (1959). Instead, he turned to writing screenplays and completed, in fairly rapid succession, the filmscript for *Tea and Sympathy* (1956); followed by *Until They Sail* (1957), based on a long story in James Michener's *Return to Paradise;* and *The Nun's Story* (1959), adapted from Kathryn Hulme's book, for which he received an Academy Award nomination. (A screen treatment of Romain Gary's *Lady L* was shelved by the producers; and a filmscript on the life of Dr. Tom Dooley that he researched in Laos in 1960 was never produced.) Anderson regards this interlude of writing for the movies not as an end in itself, but as "a crutch for me to keep busy and occupied," as something to ward off "being depressed . . . and I feel that this spell of work [gave] me a good groundwork to get back into my own work," for after Phyllis's death, "I found I didn't care about anything at all. This is what troubled me most, since a person not only can't write, but can't live very well without caring about something. My doctors said. . . . that I should work. The only thing left for me to do was a movie, which would keep me busy but on something objective."[23]

In December of 1959, Anderson married stage, screen, and television actress Teresa Wright, whom he had first met in 1951 when she acted in his adaptation of *Trilby* for the Theater Guild. In the mid-1960s, Anderson directed her in a summer stock production of *Tea and Sympathy,* and she later originated the role of the sister Alice in *I Never Sang for My Father.*

During the 1960s and early 1970s, Anderson's writing was as intensely varied as it had been during the late 1940s and early 1950s, though he has never again achieved the critical plaudits that welcomed *Tea and Sympathy.* In this period, his work included three more plays in addition to *Father*: *The Days Between,* presented by the American Playwrights Theater, on whose board of governors Anderson has served since its inception in 1964; *You Know I Can't Hear You When the Water's Running,* comprised of four short comedies; and *Solitaire/Double Solitaire* (1971), an evening of two one act plays. He also finished three other filmscripts: an original, thus far unproduced comedy entitled *A Small Part of a Long Story* (1962); and adaptations of Richard McKenna's *The Sand Pebbles* (1966) and of his own drama *I Never Sang for My Father* (1970), for which he received the Writers Guild of America Award and a second Academy nomination. Rounding out this period of his career are the intensely personal novel *After,* his first published fiction, and even a musical version of *Roman Holiday,* with lyricist-composer Richard Adler, which has never reached the stage.

Besides pursuing his own writing projects, he continued to teach — at the Salzburg Seminar in American Studies during 1968 and as writer in residence at the University of North Carolina in 1969, as well as at Harvard in 1974 and at the University of Iowa in 1975 — and to involve himself actively in organizations devoted to bettering the state of American drama and dramatists, most notably The Dramatists Guild of the Authors League of America. He has been a member of that group, founded "to define and obtain equitable rights for Dramatists," particularly their "right to maintain the integrity of their scripts against frequently enforced Managerial changes,"[24] since 1954, and served as its president from 1971–1973.

IV *Principles of Playwriting*

When asked specific questions about one or another of his plays, Anderson will ordinarily answer volubly and candidly; his written essays, however, are relatively brief and less revealing. As he once said, "I enjoy writing plays. I do not enjoy writing essays and notes about my plays."[25] So to approach his essays and expect to isolate from them anything like a systematic treatment of his own dramaturgical practice or a more generalized theory of drama places a demand upon them that their author never intended. In short, Anderson is a practicing playwright and not a theoretician. His theory — if indeed he can be said to have one — is comprised of some loosely related notions that grow out of his thirty years of experience as a playwright, and his reflections on that experience.

Despite regarding "playwrighting [as] the most difficult form of writing"[26] (yet one that compensates for this by standing its practitioners in good stead to later attempt other forms), Anderson sees the ability to write for the theater not as a gift from the muse but as a discipline and craft that can, indeed must, be learned: "There are no formulas, but there is a form. . . . This is what it takes the time and the work to absorb."[27] In other words, Anderson — perhaps because of his lengthy genesis as a dramatist and years as a teacher — puts little stock in the untutored genius who comes to playwriting without a sense of the tradition that has preceded him; if called upon to give one piece of advice to fledgling dramatists, it would be that of "the painter Renoir. . . . 'First of all, learn to be a good craftsman. This will not keep you from being a genius.'"[28]

The structure that Anderson himself mastered was that of the realistic, Ibsenite, well-made drama, a form that he has consistently employed throughout his career; even a play like *I Never Sang for My Father,* nonrepresentational in its staging and use of a narrator, belies the Ibsenite influence in its building of the conflict. Given his predisposition toward the well-made play, Anderson predictably views plot as the *sine qua non* of drama. In "Thoughts on Playwriting," his most extended (though still only a few pages in length) discussion of the nature of writing for the theater, he points out that "plot, no matter how slight, is what moves a play forward and holds our interest,"[29] so that "the climax, the moment that catches you by the throat, is still [even in the modern theater that employs 'new ways of telling a story'] a man alone on the same old high wire defying the same old law of gravity."[30] But while matters of technique, the *"How"* to structure a play, can be perfected through practice and imposed from without, the substance, or "*What* he feels, thinks, believes, loves, fears, hopes" that "finally makes the writer,"[31] is innate. What is required is that the dramatist be willing to explore himself unreservedly, to "look in his heart and write . . . with passion and conviction."[32]

Therefore, since "most plays do not come from an 'idea' or a gimmick but rather grow out of the essence of the writer,"[33] the act of playwriting is confessional in nature, fulfilling the artist's need for self-expression. "All good playwriting," Anderson believes, "is, in a sense, the dramatization of a diary. Playwriting is highly personal, not necessarily autobiographical in details, but certainly derived from the author's attitudes and points of view, which are in turn derived from his 'experience.' It seems that the better plays are becoming more and more personal."[34] Plays are, in their essentials, therefore, a kind of commonplace book of the men who write them, but with a difference: they not only record conscious thoughts, but dredge up their subconscious ones as well. Commenting on the no-holds-barred probing of his own psyche that lies at the basis of all his work, Anderson has proclaimed, "Every play I've ever written is me. I am Naked when I finish."[35]

Although Anderson cannot point to certain of his plays and say, "I dreamed them one night" (as O'Neill reputedly could of both *Desire Under the Elms* and *Ah, Wilderness!*), he has said that "Writing for me is like undoing a dream."[36] But if playwriting is dramatizing a diary or unraveling a dream, the problem becomes the age-old one of how adequately to objectify the experience to keep it from being too private: "If a playwright writes too specially about himself, and if his life hasn't got enough of universality in it, naturally it's not going to appeal to many people. It's going to be weird, neurotic, psychotic almost"[37] — a fear that never becomes a reality for Anderson as it does for Tennessee Williams in such later plays as *Out Cry.*

What of the audience's response to a play in which the dramatist has successfully universalized his own feelings? In Anderson's novel *After,* the first person narrator (who is also an authorial character) identifies the theatrical experience as communal in nature, so that one's sense of participation is "heightened by other people's awareness. The excitement of the theatre . . . . is to share, to affirm one's excitement and have it reaffirmed by the excitement of those around you."[38] The bond of solidarity exists not only between one spectator and every other spectator, or between each spectator and the play, but also between the spectator and the playwright as well, so that one's sense of isolation is replaced by a feeling of community. Echoing the words of his friend and fellow dramatist Arthur Miller, Anderson has said, "I think that one of the functions of a play is to make you feel less lonely. You go to a play and you say, 'My God, he feels that way too. It's not just me.'"[39]

Creating for the viewers the excitement of involvement in a shared experience or assuaging their loneliness springs from the dramatist's requisite obligation vis à vis his audience: to make them feel. Like his British contemporary John Osborne, who asserts "I want to make people feel, to give them lessons in feeling,"[40] Anderson has reiterated over and again: "I believe you go to the theater to be shattered into tears or excitement or something."[41] Thus he attributes the failure of much serious drama today precisely to its inability to be "deeply disturbing" to an audience, for they "don't want to see a drama and not cry or be moved by some excitement."[42]

Diametrically opposite from Bertolt Brecht's aim of estrangement, Anderson's unabashed espousal of an outward emotional response — one that sees no greater impropriety in shedding tears at a serious play than in guffawing raucously at a comic one — has definite ramifications so far as his own works are concerned. Given the aesthetic principle that says there must be some proportion between the stimulus (in this case, the play) and the response to it, it becomes clear that Anderson's chosen métier, if it is to shatter an audience into tears, will very likely often be closer to melodrama than to tragedy; this, predictably enough, has often elicited from critics such as Gerald Weales accusations of excessive sentimentality. In addition, Weales is not alone in observing that Anderson's plays sometimes verge on soap opera.[43] While it is true that Anderson's recurrent subjects — "love and sex and death and marriage"[44] — readily lend themselves to treatment in lesser modes, they can just as easily (as the history of drama documents) be the concerns of serious, even tragic, drama. To his credit, Anderson always avoids trivializing his themes, though, at the same time, he can hardly be called a philosophical or metaphysical playwright. His thematic motifs, however, are not so limited as his own list would seem to indicate, for very early in his career the list must be broadened to include such concerns as freedom versus commitment, especially as it pertains to the friction created by the opposing imperatives of self-development and obligation to others, guilt and responsibility, and adherence to ideals versus compromise.

Anderson's commitment to a drama of feelings, of sentiment, that plumbs his audience's obsessions, has exposed him to charges of casting himself in the role of therapist or analyst, and rendered his plays in the eyes of some critics, particularly Robert Brustein, little more than sensitivity sessions or imitation encounter groups. Speaking against what he sees as a growing tendency among the second rank of American playwrights who came to the fore in the 1950s to offer palliatives for the audience's ills, Brustein writes:

> Clearly, the newer American playwrights often confuse themselves with psychological counselors, for deeply imbedded in their plays you will generally find an object lesson about the diagnosis and treatment of romantic, emotional, family, or social disorders. William Gibson affirms that by charitably helping others you may absolve your own guilt; Robert Anderson tells us that adulterous encounters can be considered a form of self-sacrifice and sympathy; William Inge plumps for 'maturity' in love and family relationships; and Paddy Chayefsky suggests that romantic passion will conquer psychosis, neurosis, and evil spirits.[45]

Yet Brustein here falls prey to the intentional fallacy: Anderson and company do not provide him with the kind of play that he wants and feels philosophically comfortable with, and that he thinks America needs at this juncture (in this particular essay Brustein lauds the modern French dramatists who perform "radical surgery" rather than "feed us aspirin fantasies").

Furthermore, Anderson seems content with a less lofty role than Brustein would like all dramatists to be molded in; he writes plays for the theater and the audience, rather than for the literature collection on the library shelf; and he is generally pleased when they affect people's lives very immediately in the theater (after *Double Solitaire,* for instance, "Husbands and wives have been known to leave the theater by different doors and not see each other for several days. Husbands and wives have also spoken to each other, really spoken to each other, for the first time in years."), or when they "find extended use" as required readings in nonliterary disciplines (*I Never Sang for My Father,* for example, in courses on gerontology, or *After* in medical school colloquia on death and the survivor).[46] Susan Wittig makes a useful distinction between "popular drama" as "discourse conscious only of its message" and "artistic or esthetic drama" as "discourse conscious of itself as a made thing, a system of human signs that demand recognition as *signs,* not as natural phenomena" and that focus "our attention on *how* the drama comes to have meaning, rather than on *what* it means."[47] If we accept this explanation, it becomes clear that Anderson often settles for being a popular dramatist in the eyes of much of his audience. Yet, as is evident from his remarks on his own process of writing and as will become even more evident through a careful examination of the plays themselves, he is just as often equally an aesthetic dramatist.

Anderson feels, with some justification, especially since Inge's death, that he is the only American playwright of his generation who writes about "the normal sexual relationships between a man and woman in marriage"[48]; Williams ordinarily does, after all, portray atypical, neurotic, some would say aberrant, sexual relationships, while Miller hardly concerns himself with charting the sexual relationships of his characters at all, except in *After the Fall.* And Anderson's vision of married life, however restricted and even sometimes repetitious the terrain of the works in which it appears, is both original and individual. Just as one can speak of archetypal characters in the drama of others (the O'Neill father; the Williams woman; the Williams artist figure; the Miller father and son), so, too, one can delineate the Anderson male (often a middle-aged writer, product of unfulfilled dreams and ideals, disillusioned with life and love, yet still romantic about sex) and female (soft, sensitive, restricted in her personal development by her commitment to husband and family) that he has refracted and refined throughout a substantial body of work still not complete.

CHAPTER 2

The "Learning Plays"

WHEN offering advice to aspiring dramatists, Anderson often quotes the statistics showing that the average time that elapses between a playwright's first completed play and his first Broadway production is ten years.[1] If one counts Anderson's two dozen college plays, written between 1935 and 1941, then his period of waiting was almost twice that long; but if one considers *Come Marching Home* as his first serious effort, then the time between that and the New York opening of *Tea and Sympathy* in 1953 is somewhat shorter than the average. During that waiting period, however, three of Anderson's full length plays received at least semiprofessional productions: *Come Marching Home* was seen at the State University of Iowa, where it was directed by Hallie Flanagan and Phyllis Anderson, at the Pasadena Playhouse, and briefly at the Blackfriars Guild in New York during May 1946; *The Eden Rose* and *Love Revisited* were both performed in summer stock, the former at the Ridgefield (Connecticut) Summer Theater in 1948, the latter at the Westport (Connecticut) County Playhouse in 1951.

Because none of these three plays has been published, making them virtually inaccessible to readers of Anderson's later work, they are discussed here in detail, particularly since there is hardly a situation, character type, thematic motif, or dramatic technique in any of the better known dramas whose genesis cannot be traced back to these "learning plays," as Anderson calls them.[2] From this, one should not infer that Anderson's talent as a dramatist has not matured, but only that by the time he arrived on Broadway, at the relatively late age of thirty-six, his central concerns — the nature of idealism and the nature of marriage, and what happens to each with the passage of time — had already solidified.

I Come Marching Home

Come Marching Home — the title alludes, of course, to the popular Civil War song, "When Johnny Comes Marching Home" — is Anderson's only play that might be termed "political" in the narrow sense of that word, dealing as it does with the corruption of elected officials and the complacency of the electorate. In it, Anderson focuses on youthful idealism as it confronts a political reality that demands concessions, and ultimately capitulation, unless the idealist refuses to relinquish his function as conscience of the community and thereby chooses to assume the burden of being stigmatized as an outsider.

Predictably, such a subject prompted encomiums like "honest," "sincere," and "impassioned" in the first New York reviews Anderson received, yet the verdicts were invariably tempered with some reservations, like that of *Times* critic Louis Calta, who felt that the drama "fails to attain the theatrical forcefulness that one might expect from its provocative theme."[3] Anderson's first substantial notice, by George Jean Nathan, was considerably more severe than most, calling the play "much less drama than a forum harange": "The play, while hot with honest conviction, misses by virtue of its rabble-rouser writing and its author's inability to make its theme proceed naturally from his characters."[4] Nathan's latter contention, however, is hardly borne out by close examination of the text.

Anderson's play inevitably suffered by comparison with two other backstage political dramas, both winners of the Pulitzer Prize, that share much the same point of view: Maxwell Anderson's *Both Your Houses* (which Robert Anderson, despite his admiration for the older Anderson's work, claims never to have read[5]), and Howard Lindsay and Russell Crouse's *State of the Union,* which, while it could not have influenced Anderson, was still running on Broadway when *Marching Home* opened. Critics and public alike had also seen a similar political tale retold in such popular movies as Frank Capra's *Mr. Smith Goes to Washington.* In a letter to Nathan before the opening, Anderson admitted that he had miscalculated the public's saturation point for material of this sort: "'I thought that I was being most daring to write a post-war play, but I should have known that a nation which buys its morning paper, [sic] the night before and its Monday magazines the preceding

Thursday would be tired of the post-war theme before the war was over.'''[6]

John Bosworth, formerly a college teacher and writer (a number of the playwright's protagonists share, with Anderson himself, this dual vocation) "comes marching home" a hero from World War II, receives a tremendous public welcome arranged and sponsored by the corrupt State Senator Crawford — who knows the vote-getting value of being seen with a war hero — and quickly finds himself pitted against Crawford in the next election as a replacement for a candidate killed in an accident. Not political by nature, John's central conflict in this competently plotted if unsophisticated well-made play is the pull between his public duty on the one hand and his desire on the other to retreat into a well-deserved private world of wife and home in the country. Perfectly satisfied to rest on his Navy Cross, he envisions "not do[ing] anything important for the rest of [his] life"; he will "do some writing in the morning, putter around [his] house and grounds in the afternoon, and make love to [his] wife at night (I, i, 21)[7] — which, to the wry delight of the audience, he has almost no opportunity to do on his first night home in two years.

John's decision to divorce himself from public life stems primarily from disillusionment with a world that does not measure up to the image he developed of it at his father's knee. John's father, who had, like Anderson's, run for public office, was incurably, even naively, optimistic. Missing completely the satire that undercuts Voltaire's Dr. Pangloss (the subtitle of *Candide,* remember, is "Optimism"), the elder Bosworth literally thought that he could, simply through winning a local election, "make this the best possible world"; however, as John's mother tells it, "defeat .... killed him .... he was dead long before he died. He couldn't understand how the children of God could be so stupid and cruel. You're both innocence [sic] abroad" (II, i, 16). Returning home with a vision of war's evil, John now realizes the insufficiency of his father's facile optimism, and so tells his wife Toni that when they rear their own children, they will be more "realistic": "I don't want them to be brought up the way I was, thinking that everyone and everything is good and beautiful" (I, ii, 29). Whereas John's father had attempted to actualize perfection in and through the social order, John returns with a narrower, more achievable intention of following Voltaire's prescription to Candide to "'Cultivate your own garden,''' though that he understands the advice more narrowly than Voltaire intended becomes clear when he says: "I think if everyone made his own small part of the world as fine as possible the world would be perfect" (I, ii, 29). The restricted world into which he desires to withdraw with Toni and, someday, their children as a protection against further disillusionment is myopic in the extreme, not — as a critic of Voltaire says — "involving a larger group than the family circle, and big with promise,]as] is Candide's garden — a co-operative model society working ever so gradually, but with practical assurance, for the betterment of civilization."[8]

Aware that politics, as well as boring him, has a pragmatic and even "unattractive" side that would perpetually come up against his "damndest conscience" (I, ii, 26, 34) and his compulsion as a point of honor to always tell the truth, John fears what the outcome would be: "an idealist either becomes a cynic or goes crazy" (I, ii, 29). If he can avoid contact with the public world, perhaps his ideals will not be totally shattered. So apathy will be his buffer and excuse: "There's nothing I can do about it" (I, ii, 34).

Given John's resistance to entering the political arena — something the audience knows he eventually must do if there is to be sufficient conflict to sustain the play — Anderson builds much of Act One on the question: What will be the decisive factor in Bosworth's decision to run for office? Ostensibly, the thing that finally sways him is a series of phone calls just prior to the first act curtain threatening him with bodily harm if he accepts the nomination. Working on him more subtly and compellingly, however, is the argument of his former colleague and mentor, Professor Cunningham, who appeals sentimentally to John's remaining idealism: he must help restore integrity and truth to politics so that the hardships and sacrifices of the war will have a meaning, so that people will know what it was they fought and died to protect. John himself has less need than most others for such proof, but admits that even he was goaded on to fight partially from a less honorable motive — revenge: "It was discouraging to watch man groping for an idea or an ideal worth dying for.... Pretty soon, of course, we all lost friends, and that gave us somewhat of a personal reason" (I, ii, 28). What John comes to understand through Cunningham is his potential now to provide these men with a positive public reason instead of their basically negative personal one. If he wins office, perhaps he can counteract "all the rottenness, stupidity and greed that runs riot in this country regardless of what some poor little guy may do on a beachhead in Sicily, Italy, France, or Iwo Jima'' (I, ii, 35).

But while John campaigns to restore the faith of others in the political system, he also risks, in the process of seeing the nitty-gritty of politics, having his own faith shaken. During Act Two the question becomes: What effect will running have on John Bosworth? He enters the race with his own ideal of personal conduct intact; like "Don Quixote tilting with windmills,'' he will go before the populace with "no promises, no assurances'' (I, ii, 36). A political neophyte, he suffers from an unrealistic perception of the day-to-day workings of government, believing that since it is "the American way of doing things,'' the "best man'' unfailingly "gets the job'' despite the patronage system; and that simply telling the truth will be an "adequate defense against the charge of libel'' (II, i, 6, 8). John's undeviating honesty makes it impossible for any audience to believe for one minute that he will succumb to any attempt to secure votes through promises. Thus there is no conflict in those parts of the play where a succession of visitors arrive to tempt John's integrity. In short, Anderson has made him too good for the good of his play.

Yet if the outcome of these visits is a foregone conclusion, they are still useful to Anderson's purpose as revelations of what the electorate is like. Not only are many politicians crooked — Senator Crawford, for example, was reelected even after misappropriating funds and is running again even though under indictment for fraud, all of which must seem less bizarre today than at the time the play was written — but the people, through their complacency, contribute to that corruption. Toni tells the audience that John "felt that if he let the people know the truth about the corruption in this town, they'd see the light and overthrow the machine'' (II, ii, 26), which, of course, simply does not happen. Jaded by past experience, the people think it matters little who holds office; the electorate, John quickly discovers, is "sound asleep.'' (II, 1, 9).

In the midst of such a citizenry, John terms himself, in an allusion to Ibsen's drama, "a pillar of society'' (III, i, 1). Throughout most of Ibsen's play, Karsten Bernick is a corrupt whitened sepulchre, who only in the closing moments unconvincingly becomes what Bosworth is all along, a bastion of truth. But the drama of Ibsen's that bears the closest resemblance to Anderson's in the presentation of its central figure and the electorate is *An Enemy of the People* (which Arthur Miller would adapt for the American stage in 1950 when the country was hounded by McCarthyism). Without a doubt, John Bosworth is a descendant of Ibsen's John Stockmann, who stands alone, deserted eventually even by the liberal press, in opposition to a city administration that thinks nothing of risking people's physical health for economic gain. In words that echo not only Ibsen's sentiments but, as Michael Meyer has pointed out, those of John Stuart Mill as well, Stockmann states the case for society's need of an intellectual elite, noble in character, spirit, and will, to protect it from the collective mediocrity of majority opinion: "The majority *never* has right on its side. . . . I don't imagine you will dispute the fact that at present the stupid people are in an absolutely overwhelming majority all the world over. . . . The majority has *might* on its side — unfortunately; but *right* it has *not.* I am in the right — I and a few other scattered individuals. The minority is always in the right."[9]

John, however, is not quite a carbon copy of Stockmann; if he were, he would go too much against the American grain. Though he does, like Stockmann, suffer physical abuse at the hands of the mob, Bosworth never arrives at such an extreme antidote to society's ills as his dramatic ancestor, who finally disbelieves in democracy and arrogantly preaches a gospel of selective breeding. Indeed, Stockmann's Messiah complex, his need to become a martyr or scapegoat for society, ultimately renders him, as even Ibsen realized, a "muddled" visionary at best, reducing him, in the audience's eyes, to a serio-comic rather than an unquestionably heroic individual. In the abstract, John faces the same danger as Stockmann of becoming an arrogant elitist who regards the mass of humanity with disdain, and this, together with the danger of becoming so cynical as to fall into an absolute negativism, is the chief temptation he must resist.

If Anderson perhaps discovered a prototype for John Bosworth in Ibsen's characterization of John Stockmann, he most assuredly found examples in Ibsen's modified well-made play form for his structural pattern in *Marching Home,* in which the plot is based on a secret, only gradually revealed, that unmasks a previously held illusion — as is true, for instance, of *Ghosts,* in which Mrs. Alving thinks that she had done right in abiding by the constraints of duty and remaining with her dissolute husband rather than seeking the "joy of life." So while there is no suspense over whether Bosworth will succumb to the representatives of special interest groups who demand favors for guarantees of votes, Anderson does achieve considerable interest in Acts Two and Three over whether John will withdraw from the campaign under threat of blackmail. The muckrakers start to work. Although they can find John guilty only of having written "editorials displaying extremely radical tendencies .... for his college paper" (II, i, 13) and of having committed a minor indiscretion while drunk in London (its exact nature is left annoyingly ambiguous), John's father, it happens, "was not always scrupulous in his business dealings and what is more interesting was very susceptible to pretty faces" (II, ii, 39). One of those "pretty faces" told all to the newspaper, and the senior Bosworth bowed out of the race. Now the paper threatens finally to reveal this unless John withdraws — admittedly a circuitous chain of events on which to hinge the plot. This exposition about the father is the closest thing to a subplot in the play; in the future, Anderson will ordinarily develop such material into a double plot.

Given earlier indications that John worshipped his father, the secret, unlike the secret in a typical Ibsen play, has unbelievably little effect upon him. Unlike the idealistic young sons one finds in Miller plays, such as Chris Keller in *All My Sons* or Biff Loman in *Death of a Salesman,* who are traumatized when they discover that their fathers do not live up to the image they had of them and then feel compelled to pass judgment on the fathers for their moral failures, John unaccountably passes it off, not really caring if the paper does run the story. Yet there is nothing to suggest that he refuses to comply with the blackmail as a means of publicly tarnishing an idol who has fallen in his own eyes.

Instead of John being concerned about his father's good name, it is his mother who desires to protect the family's reputation and takes it as a *fait accompli* that John will submit to the blackmailers. That she regards John as a substitute for her late husband becomes evident from her treatment of her daughter-in-law; Toni, nevertheless, instead of rising to the bait in this potential battle between mother and wife, remains blissfully calm and sure of herself — and with good reason, since John has successfully broken from his mother's apron strings — and simply pampers her mother-in-law with small pleasures. It is not until *The Days Between* and *I'll Be Home for Christmas* two decades later that one again finds in Anderson such unfavorable characterizations of the mother; by the time Anderson writes his next produced play, *The Eden Rose,* the mother has become (and this was true of the playwright's own mother) the ideal parent, compassionate, wise, loving without being cloyingly so, while the fathers increasingly come in for criticism.

As John approaches the climactic moment of decision early in Act Three, the conflict takes on a sharper focus, very similar to the central dilemma that Gene Garrison will face, but on a more personal level, in *I Never Sang for My Father:* Where does obligation to self end and duty to others begin? What are the limits, if any, of one's social responsibility? Chet Powell, whose life John had once saved and who now offers him the veterans' votes in return for certain favors, tutors John in the value of self-interest and Dr. Belmont, who treats John after he is attacked as a fascist by the mob, joins Mrs. Bosworth in counseling personal happiness over civic duty. As a foil to them both is the latter's best friend, Mrs. Comstock, whose feisty manner adds some levity to the play. Though the object of John's denunciations for conniving to have the streetcars routed past the family department store, she offers to supply him with "any details" he lacks; to be talked about this way will be "good fun," since she has not "been gossiped about for years" (II, i, 12), which shows up the foolishness of overvaluing propriety. As is often true in Ibsen, undue emphasis on outward respectability can become a vice. Through characters like her and Joe Zaccanino, who finally reverses his earlier position and swings his support to John without assurance of patronage jobs, Anderson manages to maintain a more realistic balance than Ibsen had in *Enemy of the People* between the forces in conflict; never does Bosworth stand as alone — isolated good pitted against unmitigated evil — as Stockmann too melodramatically must in the earlier drama.

When the party decides on election eve that it must withdraw its support and nominate a politically safer candidate, John must again choose between the attractive option of retreating totally from the public arena or waging a campaign as an independent, without hope of winning, in a perpetually imperfect world, with only his wife by his side to help him when he is "most alone." In opting for the latter course, he, like Mill's and Ibsen's "aristocrats," accepts the role of gadfly, of conscience of the people. As he says in the long political oration that brings the play to a close, "though I shall be defeated, I shall be back year after year, to remind you of my friends who thought there was something here worth the trouble, the trouble to die. I shall not be afraid to be a patriot out of season" (III, ii, 18). Nevertheless, as Ibsen also realized, the possibility remains that John always will be "out of season," always one step ahead of the majority.

While learning that "there is no such thing" as a "private world" (III, ii, 19) or a perfect world, and that self-interest is normally just selfishness, John Bosworth successfully resists the temptation of indulging in negativism and cynicism, which, with their nay-saying disbelief in the potential for constructive action, are really nothing more than a reverse form of sentimentality. If his idealism is no longer as naive or quixotic as it once was, it is still intact, tempered yet fortified by experience, something that is not often true for many of Anderson's later, albeit physically older, idealists. That Bosworth retains his idealism suggests his creator's youthful outlook; that so many of Anderson's later protagonists find their illusions in tatters, with no easy curative in sight, is welcome proof of the growing maturity in outlook that *Come Marching Home* hints lies ahead.

II The Eden Rose

If, in *Come Marching Home,* Anderson focuses on the nature of idealism, with only a cursory interest in the marriage of John and Toni Bosworth, in his next produced play, *The Eden Rose,* he concentrates on exploring the nature of married love, which (with only few exceptions) becomes the pervasive subject of his dramas, filmscripts, and fiction from this point on. And idealism in *Eden Rose,* instead of being political as in *Marching Home,* appears as an immature, adolescent tendency to romanticize marriage and sex — a guise it will consistently assume in Anderson's succeeding works. *Eden Rose* is, therefore, a much more seminal play for its author's development; indeed it, and *All Summer Long* written a few years later, contain virtually every important motif appearing in his better known works written over the succeeding two and a half decades.

The most stageworthy of the three "learning plays," *Eden Rose* might well have introduced Anderson to Broadway audiences had it not been for casting difficulties; a director had been chosen, but no actress suitable for the role of Nan Hilton, a thirty-nine year old painter, was willing to undertake the central part. For although Anderson describes Nan as "appealing and attractive — definitely a man's woman — warm, human, unaffected, understanding and tender" (I, 1),[10] she not only has a twenty-year-old son and breaks society's taboo by falling in love with a man ten years her junior, but in the third act must appear without makeup — the art that prevents her from being "a very plain and dowdy woman" (I, 12). Lacking a name actress, this charming play, despite being admirable in plotting and characterization, was seen only in summer stock.

As the curtain rises, Nan is discovered with Oliver Sexton, a once married and just under fifty English professor, soon to become her fiancé for the twenty-second time in nine months. Twenty-one times before tonight they have decided to marry, only to change their minds, each broken engagement commemorated by an appropriate charm for her bracelet. According to Nan, Oliver has "talked [her] out of it" (I, 5) all those times, while he claims that it was always she "who said, 'all right, let's wait'" (I, 7). To support her interpretation, he is something of a philanderer, hardly ready to settle down again with one woman, but the responsibility for the continual postponements is probably more hers than his. Despite Nan's denial, the idea of marriage to an older man does unsettle her, for when she painted his portrait, as Oliver noticed, she "insisted on making [him] much too handsome and at least ten years younger than [he] was" (I, 8). Oliver sees her artistic temperament, her need "to create something that wasn't humdrum, pale grey sameness," as lurking behind her hesitancy to commit herself to a marriage that she knows will be essentially placid and "not blaze into a great fire" (I, 8). Although Nan denies being one of Oliver's "passionate heroines with a smouldering soul" and asserts her readiness to settle for a union of "wonderful companionship" and "contentment" (I, 12, 9), Oliver senses that her secret definition of herself includes "a touch of Lady Chatterley in it" (I, 13). The real wellspring of her character, whether she realizes it or not, is her as yet unfulfilled sexuality.

If she has repressed this aspect of her personality, it is partially because of attitudes toward sex formed during adolescence, as well as the relatively cold nature of her first marriage, in which she evidently had to be content with something less than the man of a young girl's dreams. Her first husband, Tom Hilton — a naval officer killed in the war a year before the play opens — was an incommunicative, "self-sufficient" man who never made Nan feel "needed" (I, 32). Anderson suggests that the contraint and gulf between them was more than a product of geographical separation by Nan's hesitancy to send Tom "a book of poetry, a rather earthy book of love poems" that she had bought for him but "then decided he wouldn't like" (I, 30–31). Finding the thought of youthful rebellion and defiance "exciting," she had married without her family's consent, revealing: "We might never have been married if they had approved" (II, 30). Seeing Tom as an opportunity to escape a sheltered, restrictive existence, she did not "wait for a great love" but took "whatever there was in the present" (III, 16); so the passion, never adequately fed in her, dried up sooner than it might have. Now Nan, not yet forty, wants to believe that it is too late for rekindling sexual feeling in her life. She feels ripe, therefore, for a platonic marriage to Oliver.

For him, love and sex are easily divisible. Caring for a person — his kindness to Nan in her loneliness, for instance — and feeling sexual passion toward that person do not ordinarily coincide: "it's years really," he confesses to Nan, "since I've cared for anything or anyone sufficiently to get that worked up over it" (III, 25). Yet, functioning as Anderson's raissoneur, he knows the insufficiency of this philosophy as a foundation for marriage, in which love and sex, care and passion must fuse. This view is a central motif in the plays of Philip Barry, whom Anderson cites as a major influence on his work. In Barry's *Paris Bound,* for instance, the raissoneur James Hutton, whose wife Helen divorced him because he had an affair, argues that he "may have committed adultery . . . but [he] never committed divorce. . . . *our* province [that is, his love for Helen within marriage which he defines as 'a spiritual relationship which belonged only to us'] was never touched by it."[11] There can be sex without love, but a satisfactory marriage cannot be built on love without sex.

What Oliver offers Nan is "calm sublimity" in a union where "the tensions of great passions are missing"; they will drift peacefully into the future, living out their "long autumn years" in "a couple of rockers reserved at a lonely little summer hotel called with great originality *The Breezes*" (I, 11; III, 25–26). When Oliver mentions his inability to "any longer play the role of dependable old Charlie" in relation to Nan (II, 10), he is alluding verbally to Charlie Marsden in O'Neill's *Strange Interlude,* who, unlike Sexton in that he has passed beyond desire, offers Nina Leeds a time of tranquility in a union without "passion and possession to wither the heart with bitter poisons."[12] Oliver realizes, however, that the time has not come for Nan to drift into this sort of relationship with him; she has not yet experienced her interlude of passion. He would be offering Nan the autumn and eventually the winter before she had tasted the summer. Nan understands that "change is common to all things and people" (III, 17), but in her decision to settle down with Oliver, she attempts to hasten time's process, and that in a drama where the need for a proper understanding of and respect for time is a dominant motif.

In this play, structured in terms of the Hegelian thesis-antithesis-synthesis, Oliver and Nan's potentially platonic love, predicated solely on a union of mind rather than body, is the first element of the Hegelian triad. The second, or antithesis, is the love between Nan's son Roger, a college student whose avocation (like Anderson's own in his youth) is music, and twenty-eight year old Madge Wilson, whom Roger met just after his father's death. Theirs is a wholly physical love. Evidently Nan served as her son's confidante and advisor even before Tom's death, understandably, given Tom's absence during the war and his inner-directed personality; even so, strongly implied is a lack of companionship and communication between father and son. As is true not only of Anderson's own mother but of a number of the mothers in his plays, it was Nan who instructed Roger in the facts of life, Fortunately for him — as Oliver, who "learned quite differently," is the first to point out — Nan was not only "quite detailed" but also "tried to make it something quite beautiful" rather than sordid (I, 18). Although, as Nan says, "it seems terribly illogical, [that] men always tell men about women" (II, 29), Anderson does not necessarily intend to overturn the traditional notion that fathers should be responsible for the sex education of their boys, just so one parent does it frankly yet sensitively. Perhaps Nan so conscientiously and lovingly fulfilled this duty because of her own unsatisfactory training, inferred from her making a "small soap carving" of the Venus de Milo — without a bosom": "I was only 12 or 13 when I did it — and I was a little embarrassed about bosoms — and things" (I, 26).

While Roger perceives that the basically unemotional relationship between Nan and Oliver contains little of what his mother has always told him should hold true of marriage, this assurance that their life together will be "quite platonic" (II, 3) paradoxically has a soothing effect on Roger, freeing him from the embarrassment that many immature children feel at the thought of their parents passionately in love. If Roger is unlike Richard Miller in *Ah, Wilderness!,* whose "face is transfigured by a smile of shy understanding and sympathy" when he realizes that his parents once loved as intensely as he thinks he now does,[13] he is similar to most of the children in Anderson's works who jealously guard as the province of youth the experience of being "gloriously and passionately in love" (II, 31), as he is with Madge, considering such emotion as something denied to middle-aged parents. As Booth Tarkington wrote, "Youth cannot imagine romance apart from youth."[14] For Roger and Madge, only "a continuous display of fireworks" will satisfy (III, 7). Nan's dilemma over Roger's engagement is her fear that his love for Madge, based as it is on a physical attraction subject to time's vagaries, might not long endure. At the same time, though not a terribly astute judge of what she herself needs at this point in her life, she has sufficient prescience to blame herself as one source of Roger's immature idealization of physical attraction at the expense of deeper feelings.

Although Roger claims that "all that matters [is] if you really love a person" (II, 16), the falsity of his protestations becomes evident in that he and Madge have already made contingency plans for when her beauty fades: Madge will either be "adored or abandoned," there will be no half measures; "she's insisted," Roger says, "that if I ever stop loving her, really loving her, that we call it off" (II, 34–35). Nan senses that things will not be so simple, that they probably will not stop loving each other at the same time, and even if they did, it would not be without recriminations on both sides. Faced with Roger's repeated insistence that he will remain unaffected by Madge's aging faster than he, Nan adopts the best counterstrategy at her disposal; she will show Roger how she, at thirty-nine, looks without makeup, a ploy that achieves the desired effect. Roger leaves behind the engagement ring when he goes from Nan's boudoir. He learns from her a lesson that she had learned from her mother: it is sometimes the most loving gesture for the man to have "the courage .... to take leave," that Madge will come to appreciate his sacrifice in saying goodbye and "love him the rest of her life" for doing so (III, 9).

So a marriage of the physical without the spiritual has been found as wanting in the integration essential for growth as a marriage of minds that ignores the active participation of the body. The answer lies, then, in a synthesis of the two, in one that, as in the Shakespearean ideal, does not discount the physical side of man but sees the necessity for an admixture of the spiritual. In *The Eden Rose,* the relationship between Nan and her deceased husband's best friend, Ted Jones, a twenty-nine year old navy man who served on Tom's ship during the war, carries the greatest potentiality for achieving this fusion.

Because of the disparity in age between Nan and Ted (Phyllis Anderson was also ten years older than Robert), the Roger-Madge relationship becomes a double plot that parallels, except in its resolution, the main conflict of the play. Anderson is inordinately fond of counterpointing main and double or subplots, so much so that this structural technique becomes one of the earmarks of his dramaturgy. He might have discerned models for this admittedly very common practice in the plays of any number of dramatists influential upon him: in Barry's *Paris Bound,* already mentioned, Jim and Mary Hutton's marriage, as well as the two triangles involving Mary, Jim, and Noel Farley, and Jim, Mary, and Richard Parish, parallel the marriage of his parents James and Helen, but with an opposite resolution since the younger couple remains married instead of divorcing as the older couple had; or in Noel Coward's *Private Lives,* two couples on their honeymoons meet and rediscover love with their former marriage partners; or in William Inge's *Come Back, Little Sheba* (not produced until 1950 but which Anderson had read around the time he was writing *Eden Rose*) in which Lola and Doc see in Marie and Turk romanticized, idealized images of what they had always hoped the other would be.[15] It is not until Anderson writes the sketch entitled "The Footsteps of Doves" and, still later, the long one act play *Double Solitaire* — which, to be precise, employs the triple plot — that he again uses the double plot as adroitly as in *Eden Rose.*

Ted, like Oliver a teacher, recalls Anderson himself in his decision not to complete his graduate degree after coming home from the war; that he feels "tired of rummaging through wormeaten manuscripts tracing the history of the comma" (I, 22) reflects

Anderson's own sentiments about scholarly endeavors at the time and is symptomatic of a general malaise. Ted's horoscope, describing him as "a wanderer, restless, a perfectionist and essentially lonely" (I, 25), accurately limns his postwar disorientation; he is desperate for "something to happen .... almost .... anything .... that will start something going" in either his head or his heart to get him back in touch with life and help him regain his bearings (I, 29).

Like Roger, Ted is also an idealist when it comes to women, searching for one who embodies all the things he must find in a woman; love he regards as the only available source of "a wonderful and rare equilibrium in an unbalanced world" (II, 21). Love must be everything that it was not for his parents. Ted's father, not unlike Tom Hilton, was aloof and undemonstrative when it came to expressing physical affection; he "never .... touch[ed] her gently or kiss[ed] her, except an occasional peck on the cheek" (I, 31), and so Ted considers it his "father's fault" that his mother withdrew into herself, becoming cold and "unsentimental" (I, 28). Because of his parents' strained emotional relationship, Ted quickly understands the disappointing nature of Tom and Nan's marriage; perhaps, too, Ted at first finds in Nan a surrogate for the maternal warmth and affection his mother lacked. Whereas Ted feels deficient in what he has to offer any woman, Nan, doubting that she could ever be loved for herself instead of for what she can do *for* Ted, insists that his "loneliness is a lot to offer a woman. ... It gives a woman a feeling she's needed" (I, 32). Anderson's characters, both male and female, often need to be needed, but typically his women turn that need into a potentially hazardous romantic notion that marriage is a relationship in which to administer a dose of motherly solicitude. As Ted suggests in a passage that contains the germ for several later Anderson plays, loneliness and need, both within marriage and without, are a pervasive human condition waiting to be assuaged: "If all a woman wants is a lonely man, she won't have to look far. She'll find a lot of them among the married men, too. I was in a bar once at home, and I heard a familiar voice in the next booth pouring out his disappointments and heartbreaks to a two dollar woman. It was my father." To which Nan adds, "And your mother waiting at home wishing to God he'd tell her all about it" (I, 32).

Nan, without makeup, tests the depth of Ted's love, certain that he will fail as Roger did. In contrast to other well-made plays in which the long-kept secret is a letter from the past or a ghost in the family closet, the secret in *Eden Rose* is Nan herself, unadorned by cosmetics. Yet, while Ted's face "looked the same" as Roger's had, belying his shock, he does not, as Nan "expected" he would, "turn and run" (III, 16). Nan realizes Ted does "love deeply" now, but someday, when he can no longer exclaim of her "You're beautiful," she fears he will "hate" with the same intensity (III, 14). She will rest satisfied in always thinking of him as her "Eden Rose," whose "scent" need be experienced "just once" for the "enchantment" to endure (III, 18). Here, later than she expected, is the great love she never found in her youth. But Nan considers the memory more attractive than marriage to Ted would be, since the latter might falter with the passage of time.

Yet this is nothing more than Nan's own romantic pose: she desires to play the role of a woman forever cut off from consummating the great love of her life, who settles for and pines away in a marriage of companionship sustained by the pangs of unrequited love. She protects herself against the death of the dream by never allowing it to become a reality that can die. As Ted perceives, Nan is as "incurably romantic" as her mother was (III, 18). Ted, however, differs from Roger in being both more mature and less romantic, even to the point of admonishing Nan that "we're not lovers in a story-book romance to be wrenched apart in the end to give the public a catch in the throat. We're real people, Nan, who have to go on living tomorrow and the next year. Don't romanticize this, Nan" (III, 21). He promishes her not "a gilt-edged assurance of the future," or a "happily ever after," but "hate as well as love," because of his "juvenile ways .... enthusiasms, the fight I've still got ahead of me before I get anywhere" (III, 23) — all the things one risks as a part of the process of growth and change. Unconvinced, Nan sends Ted away. As he leaves, he gives her the fake wedding cake, telling her to "use it for your wedding" (III, 23), as a visual symbol to both her and the audience of the falsity of her proposed marriage to Oliver, which will deny her passionate side. Their marriage would be "static and dead," grimly life-denying rather than gloriously life-affirming, a "sit[ting] out of the rest of the dance" that is life (III, 22–23). Though it is one more twist of plot than the play needs, the audience probably is not too surprised — and assuredly is pleased — that Nan ultimately rejects

Oliver for Ted, since this resolution was foreshadowed visually when Nan earlier felt no compunction to "sit out the dance." At the end of Act One, she and Ted dance to a favorite song of theirs, and "then they are in each other's arms, the years of frustration, loneliness and secret longing suddenly released as they kiss" (I, 38). As the final curtain falls, they are once again beginning to dance, flinging themselves into what Oliver calls "the reckless mazurka of life" (III, 27). The dance, as in Shakespearean comedy and romance, is a festive ritual symbolizing and celebrating the principle of regeneration and rebirth, in this instance the birth of the marriage union out of the old separateness, the synthesis of body and soul, passion and spirit, in the marriage of Nan and Ted. Those Greek street musicians playing romantic music outside Nan's window at the opening curtain were for Nan and Ted all along.

Although Oliver acts as tutor to Nan, prodding her into an awareness of the necessity of integrating sex and love, he ironically delays the fusion within his own life; a wise counselor of others, he appears the eternal adolescent insofar as his own sexual behavior is concerned. Unable to "quite see settling down yet," he tells Nan about embarking anew on his rites of spring, perhaps so she will not feel guilty over the sacrifice he has made that allows the Lady Chatterley in her to be finally fulfilled. Upon leaving, he presents her with yet another charm to commemorate their final broken engagement: "It is shaped like a rosebud, and around the bottom of the cup is engraved in very small letters the obvious quotation about rosebuds. Robert Herrick. 17th century" (III, 26). The engraving reads, of course, "Gather ye rosebuds while ye may" — an admonition to Nan to seize this moment of great passion proffered her by Ted before it really does become too late, as she had thought for most of the play that it already was.

Yet *Eden Rose* is not merely a carpe diem play. Anderson is saying, along with the writer of *Ecclesiastes,* "To everything there is a season." Nan, afraid that the reality of her life would never measure up to the romantic dream of her youth, violated time; she speeded up time's process, making believe that the time for passion — which she sadly had never experienced with her first husband — was irrevocably past, hoping to obliterate the desire for it from her life. In her desire to move effortlessly and painlessly into the tranquility of the future, she almost missed out on the possibility for completion and growth in the present through marriage to Ted.

Time brings not only decay, but fulfillment as well. Some later Anderson heroines, particularly Barbara Potter in *Double Solitaire,* who think that the time for passion as a part of married love is past will not be so fortunate as Nan.

III Love Revisited

Among Anderson's produced plays, *Love Revisited* — which, like *The Eden Rose* was performed only briefly in summer stock — stands as the author's only attempt at writing a comedy of manners in the traditional mode established by the Restoration dramatists and kept alive in the twentieth century by such favorite playwrights of Anderson as Noel Coward and Philip Barry. *Love Revisited* remains also, among the works of a dramatist who prides himself on his ability to structure a well-made play and who does not object to being labeled a "constructionist,"[16] the least successful of Anderson's plays in both the conception and the execution of its cluttered plot. There will later be dramas — most notably *Silent Night, Lonely Night* and *The Days Between* — in which he will take calculated risks in the conception of the plot, with the result that he mistakenly gauges the viability of the structure he settles upon and its effect upon an audience. Yet in those plays, once he determines what his structural pattern will be, he executes it meticulously. But in writing *Love Revisited,* Anderson either had no firm idea of what his central plot would be and so diffuses it in several directions; or, as seems more likely, he had not developed his ability to see through the complexities (it is a play with more incidents than almost any other he has written) to the pattern behind them. Nevertheless, *Love Revisited* displays a tremendous advance in Anderson's awareness of the potentiality to convey meaning through visual stage symbols. And since *Love Revisited* is the playwright's first extended examination of what happens to a man and woman within marriage as the years pass — a favorite concern — it retains, despite its obvious flaws, more than cursory interest.

If *Eden Rose* dramatizes the prologue to a marriage, with a few hints as to what Nan and Ted's life will be like during their first years together, *Love Revisited,* which occurs on the fourteenth anniversary of Charles and Liz Webster, is late Act One of the story: the first act curtain is upon them, and in the balance lies the nature of their marriage in their middle years — the period of a marriage that Anderson most often treats in his later works. Anderson, as David H. Ayers has noticed (but without postulating any reason for it), displays a penchant for having the action in his works occur on or around some celebratory occasion:[17] in *Come Marching Home,* it is the homecoming after the war; in *Eden Rose,* Ted's birthday and the engagement; and now, in *Love Revisited,* the wedding anniversary — an especial favorite of Anderson's. In some later plays it will again be the anniversary (*Tea and Sympathy, Days Between, Double Solitaire*), whereas in others it will be a birthday (*All Summer Long*), Christmas (*Silent Night*), or, if only in illusion, Father's Day (*Solitaire*), while in the screenplays the religious profession (*The Nun's Story*) or the wedding (*Until They Sail, The Sand Pebbles*), and in his fiction (*After*) the actress's opening night, occur. Sometimes, rather than a joyful celebration, it is a sorrowful family occasion, particularly some kind of leave taking: the going away from home in *I'll Be Home for Christmas, Nun's Story,* and *Until They Sail;* or the death and funeral in *I Never Sang for My Father* and *After.* In every instance, happy or sad, the celebration of these rites is a time for taking stock, for assessing where one has been in the past, what one's present condition is, and the direction one will take in the future. These recurrent rituals, usually secular rather than religious, are visual community affirmations of man's acceptance of the cycle of birth-growth-decay-death and of his capacity for rebirth, for beginning anew.

For Liz Webster in *Love Revisited,* her fourteenth anniversary, rather than a celebration of renewal, is a moment of crisis, of deciding whether or not, in the words of Mrs. Potter in *Double Solitaire,* any "grounds exist for staying married."[18] That she traditionally observes the occasion with a nostalgic "Do You Remember Party?" hints that the reality never fulfilled the expectation, that secretly she longs to reverse time to the way things were on that day in 1936 and start all over again. Yet if, in years past, Liz was content to satisfy her longings for another chance by indulging in a one-night costume party "in which everyone]got] dressed up in the clothes of the period when we were married" (I, 3),[19] this year her discontent has grown so overpowering that she decides to play a more serious game, taking the pretense several steps farther by denying that the marriage ever existed, retreating totally into the past by feigning amnesia. Hers is a different version of violating time's process from Nan Hilton's, with whose deemphasis on the physical in love she sharply disagrees. Following an example she read about in the paper of a woman who used a similar ploy so that "her husband had to court her all over again" before he "won her back" (I, 14), Liz manages to have herself hit on the head with a copy of Ovid's *Art of Love* — the lexicon of all the sensual elements she feels are lacking in her marriage.

Now, despite her awareness that "there's something wrong when you have to go back to old songs, old memories to drum up some sort of feeling in the present" (I, 12), she can call up Nick Peterson, the sculptor with whom she lived before marrying Charles, and continue the relationship as if her husband had never happened along. But while time past can be remembered, it cannot be recaptured since it did not stand still. Nick now wears a toupee; and the brass bed he and Liz shared has long since broken. So Nick understands the workings of time better than Liz, and cautions her that, analogous to the adult who rereads a book or resees a movie he loved as a child only to find that the magic has evaporated, "love revisited" is "a dangerous business" (II, 16). He was after all only "adequate" sexually with Liz, and "not naughty" as she has falsely romanticized (II, 13). Better, he suggests, to let sleeping dreams lie rather than chance killing them with too much reality. Dramaturgically, nothing much comes of their rendezvous, except the opportunity to drag down from the attic and place conspicuously in the garden one of the two central visual symbols in the play — a three-quarter life size nude statue of Liz that Nick once sculpted. On stage during the last two acts, it functions significantly as a reminder of the physical side of marriage that Charles has lately been sadly neglecting.

Complicating the tricks Liz fabricates is the plan of their live-in relative, Aunt Emily, a delightfully eccentric busybody and Anderson's most original comic character until Richard Pawling in *The Shock of Recognition* fifteen years later. Her favorite hobby is attending funerals armed with obituary columns and bringing home stray musicians to accompany her while she plays an enormous harmonica. Working under the assumption that jealousy makes the heart grow fonder, Emily brings a young pianist, the first of two characters in the Anderson canon to bear the name Jack Barnstable (the other is the playwright in *The Shock of Recognition*), into the home with the express purpose of his playing Iago to Charles's Othello.

A bit of a hedonist, Jack willingly agrees to Emily's plot, not just to see what has become of a former radical like Charles whom he had idolized, but also because he is not above entering into a liaison with Liz — or, if he cannot snatch away the wife, then with Charles's secretary Flora. Unfortunately, from a dramatic point of view, as Emily makes explicit to an audience which is probably one step ahead of her, "with Nick coming, [Jack is] almost unnecessary" to the plot (III, 4) — both hers and Anderson's; and Jack's own ruse to add a Pirandellian touch by forcing Liz to wonder if perhaps she *really* is suffering from amnesia by claiming that she does not remember the affair they have been having for the past two years is only a superfluous box within a box. If Anderson had characterized Liz so that she did, in Pirandellian fashion, lose the ability to distinguish between the illusion and the reality, between the play-acted amnesia and the truth, then Jack's ploy would have carried some dramatic weight and added another level of confusion and comedy. But as it is, it is simply a pale repetition of the original game. Equally distracting to the audience is the inconsistency with which Liz maintains her pose of amnesia.

The play opens, however, not with Liz's assessment of the crisis in her marriage and her program for dealing with it, but rather with Charles's disillusionment over the crisis he faces in his vocation as a hack writer of radio soap operas, which provide their female listeners the vicarious "excitement, sentiment, thrills . . . Love" that help "make up for the deficiencies of civilized life and lazy husbands" (I, 9). Dissatisfied with his work since he "ran out of original ideas ten years ago" (I, 6), Charles overestimates his courage in having the word "sex" spoken over the airwaves, finding in this daring action a resurgence of the old radicalism that highlighted his youth, just as it had John Bosworth's. Charles stands as a forerunner of the playwright Jack Barnstable in *The Shock of Recognition,* who believes that having an actor appear naked on stage will be a significant gesture in the annals of the theater. Though his gesture is tamer, Charles regards himself as taking "a pioneering step" in "getting radio out of diapers" through the one novel line he has penned in years: "'our love is just . . . well, just sex'" (I, 7–8). From Liz's point of view, would that it were more true of their marriage, since Charles has downplayed the necessity for the physical expression of love. (Interestingly enough, Charles's line forms an apt prophecy of the debilitated relationships of certain later Anderson couples that are built on "just sex," particularly that of Charley and Barbara in *Double Solitaire.*)

Set in contrast to the high ideals Charles once held, Liz perceives the shallowness of his current accomplishment and sees how far he has fallen from the days of being a legend in his own time; Jack reports that people still "talk about him down in Greenwich Village and up at Yale," where he was "put in jail for leading the riot protesting the firing of the two liberal professors" (I, 33). As if to remind Charles of the demise of his former glory, Liz resurrects from the attic for this year's "do you remember party" his red blazer with "the Coat of Arms" of the "Young Liberals for Action" emblazoned on the breast pocket — a piece of attire Charles now emphatically considers "ridiculous" (I, 9), since it is a painful reminder to him of the disparity between youthful idealism and middle-aged compromise. So this play, even though comic, has a darker undertone than the preceding plays and becomes the first in a long line of Anderson works (*All Summer Long, Days Between, I'll Be Home for Christmas,* and *Double Solitaire* are some others) about the disillusionment that results from knowing one has failed to achieve what he had aspired to.

Before he married Liz, Charles had intended "to go over and fight on the side of the loyalists" in the Spanish Civil War, and it was that image of him with which Liz fell in love; just his vision of heroic feats without any validation in fact was enough to turn her from Nick to him. The burden falls on Charles to somehow live up to that image — a herculean task that ends with his compensating for his failure by showering her with material things. Now, perhaps unfairly after all these years, she demands something deeper from him as a writer after settling for so long for so little, and Charles does, too. Disgusted with the commercial dross he regularly churns out, he secretly wishes he would be fired, for he lacks "the courage to quit" on his own (I, 4), afraid of venturing into something new and beginning over again in middle age without security. Yet he may be forced to do just that, since the radio producer, Mr. Farnsworth, finds that Charles has grown cold and "sluggish" in his job — just as Liz finds him to be in his marriage — and "could use a little of [his] former rebelliousness" (III, 16). Thus Charles's puny act of daring unfortunately pleases rather than dismays Farnsworth.

Anderson's play, however, skirts any kind of resolution to this conflict over vocation; in fact, for most of the time the audience probably forgets it entirely, since the playwright fails to link dramatically the crisis in vocation with the crisis in marriage. Such a link readily exists — Charles has allowed his writing to become hackneyed just as he has permitted his marriage to go stale — but Anderson seems to think that resolving the conflict in the marriage is enough. Furthermore, Liz and Charles Webster, unlike David and Barbara Ives a decade later in *Days Between* (in many ways, a rewritten version of the earlier play in an appropriately more serious vein), do not themselves see that the two crises are interlocked. Perhaps Anderson's major miscalculation here was to think that the comedy of manners conventions he adopts for *Love Revisited* were suitable for the material; or perhaps, at this stage in his own career, having written plays for several years but without any material success to show for it, he fears probing into Charles's failure as an artist, knowing that to do so might raise serious doubts about his own choice of vocation.

As a writer, Charles recoils from assuming the role of the wronged husband that both Liz's plot with Nick and Aunt Emily's with Jack would force him into, for "In literature, the wronged husband is a comic and pathetic character held up to ridicule and scorn" (II, 38). On the other hand, Liz more than willingly assumes the traditionally sympathetic role of the wronged wife, and with some justification. Not that Charles has ever been unfaithful to her; as Emily perceives, he is too "scared" to "do anything more than flirt" with his secretaries (I, 18). Significantly, his dance with Flora in Act III, which they both suspect might be a prelude to something more, is abortive. Yet Liz does suffer from benign neglect. To Charles, "getting and keeping" suffice; his determination to live by the law of the jungle and "defend what is rightly his" prompts Nick's accusation that Charles sees marriage only as a relation of "the possessor and the possessed" (II, 39). Nick knows Liz and Charles's marriage for what it is: empty form without real substance. And the certainty that the form will always be there, unthreatened, has made Charles cocksure and apathetic: "Think how hard husbands and wives would have to work to keep their spouses loving them if the law didn't guarantee them what passes for love" (II, 42). To prevent such complacency, Mrs. Farnsworth, who has divorced her husband, proposes the unorthodox and forward-looking (for the time of the play's composition) solution that "the marriage contract ought to be like your other contracts: renewable every year contingent on the mutual satisfaction of the parties concerned" (III, 17). From Liz's angle of view, the essence of the marriage — the romance, the excitement, the physical intimacy — is missing. As would have been the case had Nan married Oliver in *Eden Rose,* Liz's union with Charles is founded only on contentment, and "Maybe contentment isn't the proper goal in marriage. There's something sedentary and final about that word" (I, 11).

Among all of Anderson's women characters, Liz holds a unique position — shared possibly only by Laura in *Tea and Sympathy;* for, by and large, Anderson believes that it is the men and not, as is stereotypically assumed, the women who are the real romantics in marriage. Although no marriage can long survive without the physical intimacy Liz wants, neither can it survive without developing some deeper bases than just a romanticized idealization of sex. So Liz in *Love Revisited* suffers from as immature a notion of the basis for a successful marriage as did Nan Hilton when she toyed with marrying Oliver. And, as with Nan also, the core of Liz's problem lies in a faulty understanding of man's proper relationship with time. Liz does not see the impossibility of erasing fourteen years from her life either through the amnesia game with Nick, or through her sentimental desire to begin married life anew with Charles as bride and bridegroom. Unsuccessful in her first attempt at "Lover Come Back to Me" (the original title of the play) with Nick, she embarks on a second try with Charles.

The climax of *Love Revisited,* nevertheless, marks a significant advance in Anderson's talent as a dramatist, for he signals the resolution for the audience wholly through a visual technique involving the two most prominent symbolic stage properties in the play: Charles, now wearing the old red blazer he earlier threw off, lovingly moves toward the nude statue of Liz and "reaches out tentatively as though maybe to touch the figure" before which candles have burnt like so many votive lights (III, 17–18). He realizes now what Liz sees as his part in the destruction of the marriage, attributing it, at least indirectly, to the success syndrome, to the perverted materialism Wordsworth had in mind when he wrote, "Getting and keeping we lay waste. . . ." By the final curtain, Charles has been converted to Liz's side. He signals his willingness to join with her in turning back the clock and beginning all over again by doing something he has not done since before their marriage: writing her a love letter filled with purple prose that calls attention to the rapidity of his change and thus reduces the play's ending to sentimentality. He writes: "I resolve to keep our marriage different. To keep it a growing thing, and not let it dwindle into stale familiarity. . . . I sort of feel that things are beginning for us, not a New Year's Eve, but a New Life's Eve, for both of us. Our life together" (III, 28–29). Charles seems to have totally forgotten the crisis he is undergoing as a writer.

If their reconciliation appears a bit too easy and painless to be believable, it is only the first of a number of such reconciliations in Anderson's plays. Yet unlike those later happy endings that might be faulted for being improbable and unearned, Liz and Charles's — demanded by the expectations of the comic form that has always made allowances for contrivances to bring the action to a close — suffers less from being improbable than from accepting an unsatisfactory basis on which to build, or in this case rebuild, a solid marriage. Though the playwright evidently considered this a happy ending, if one looks probingly and critically, it is muted at best. One senses that this union will never mature, built as it is only on the romanticized notion, staunchly rejected by all of Anderson's later, more mature heroines, that superficial things like physical attraction and an idealized notion of what life can be like together if one only has sex are enough to make a marriage work. The very bases on which Liz and Charles attempt to rebuild their marriage are precisely the things that will tear apart the marriage of David and Barbara in *Days Between* or of Charley and Barbara in *Double Solitaire.* And so *Eden Rose* gives one a clearer indication of Anderson's mature ideas about marriage than does *Love Revisited.*

If *Love Revisited* is a detour from the playwright's commonly held notions about marriage, it is also a digression, and a not very successful one, in form. Only once again, in *You Know I Can't Hear You When the Water's Running,* will Anderson write a play comic in both structure and tone — and that not in the comedy of manners genre, which is evidently not a very comfortable one for him, partially because he is not a master of witty, epigrammatic language. About the best he can muster in that vein is Liz's retort to Nick when he tells her about his wife's solicitous care of her statue — "I don't know as I like to think of my rival running a dust rag over my torso" (II, 16) — or Nick's a page later: "My uncle married my aunt for strictly platonic reasons and they had ten kids" (II, 17). After writing *Love Revisited,* Anderson might be saying, in the words of Gay Esterbrook, that fictional writer of trivial if "gallant and witty" comedy from S. N. Behrman's play of the same name, "No time for comedy." For he now turns to writing the two serious dramas that will firmly establish his reputation as a mature American playwright.

CHAPTER 3

The Maturation Plays

WHEN *Come Marching Home* played briefly in New York, several reviewers hailed Anderson as a "promising" new playwright; it would be almost seven years, however, before any considerable number of theatergoers would see the fulfillment of that promise, with the production early in 1953 of *All Summer Long* (adapted from Donald Wetzel's 1950 novel, *A Wreath and a Curse*) at Washington's Arena Stage. That play, along with *Tea and Sympathy* — which reached Broadway a year before *Summer* finally did and which still remains the playwright's most widely known work — marks Anderson's coming of age as a dramatist, as a mature artist of the theater. And strangely enough, these two plays, each of which shows the influence of one of the two dominant modes of modern drama, are both about maturation: the first a Chekovian play about a young boy entering adolescence, the second an Ibsenite play about a young man entering adulthood.

It is not difficult to understand why Anderson "love[d]" and "was deeply moved" by Wetzel's novel,[1] and why he would gravitate toward it as a source for a play, for it tells the story of a family similar to Anderson's own: the authoritarian, emotionally reserved father; the sensitive, compassionate mother; the brothers who are the closest of friends rather than sibling rivals. Since it must have struck the playwright as something akin to a fictionalized autobiography, it can be called a seminal book for Anderson. It acted as a catalyst that helped crystalize the disparate threads from the apprentice plays that would constitute his enduring concerns as an artist: the testing of idealism, disillusionment over dreams denied, the marriage between two people emotionally unsuited for one another, the father-son conflict, the mother-son symbiosis. For these reasons, and because it illuminates Anderson's methods in adapting a work from one medium into another — either from fiction into drama as he does here or from fiction into film as he will often do later — it seems appropriate to examine briefly Wetzel's metaphysical novel, and then the process by which Anderson molds the material into a play.

I *Donald Wetzel's* A Wreath and a Curse

Twenty year old Don, the first person narrator of Wetzel's novel, which takes its title from Neitzsche's admonition beginning "Slew ye not my youth's visions and dearest marvels," is a former captain of his high school basketball team now adjusting to his new condition of paralysis. Wetzel characterizes Don — who coincidentally bears the same name as Anderson's older brother — as an introspective questioner, musing speculatively in an often convoluted stream of consciousness about the "whys" of life. Less fortunate than Housman's "Athlete Dying Young," who traded a perishable crown and "fields where glory does not stay" for an "unwithered garland" of lasting, if limited, fame, Don has exchanged the memory of the wreath for the curse of being crippled: in his case, "the name died before the man," and his days of glory — both those achieved and those only dreamed of — are behind him. So his psychic and emotional wounds outweigh the physical ones. Though not impotent, Don doubts he will ever be physically attractive to a woman. Knowing his body will never again function normally and thinking himself denied the emotional fulfillment due him as a man, the rest of his life stares him in the face as a grim anticlimax, a succession of days of regret doused with self-pity.

His once active body now largely immobilized, Don must increasingly live life cerebrally; physical deprivation can, however, become a necessary precondition for increased mental awareness. "Dead" from the waist down, Don finds himself uniquely able to experience not merely "a simultaneous perception of the dead and of the living, which is common enough . . . but an actual simultaneous experience of being alive and being dead" (70).[2] But Don's periods of introspection easily fall into somber brooding over what dark purposefulness — or purposelessness — rules man's fate. Two pivotal characters, since they offer Don alternative philosophical stances, are his mother and his brother-in-law Harry. Bereft of faith in anything but his machines, Harry must reduce all experience to manageable empirical phenomena, but in so doing he risks perpetrating "the ultimate obliteration of all things that lived and had meaning as more than fact" (153). Professing this facile and comfortable religion of fact, there can be for Harry no unexplainable mystery in life that cannot be accounted for by "The great God Math. One and one make two, and all things that cannot be demonstrated and proved with this kind of incontrovertible finality are not to be trusted" (17). An equally unviable alternative, though one more sympathetically viewed from Don's embittered perspective, is his mother's uncomplicated and unwavering belief that the inexplicable ways of God to man are somehow working for man's eventual good: "surely God lived and was good and knew what was best and helped us if only we knew it and sometimes heard our prayers" (173).

In the psychomachia he undergoes, Don finds his mother's homespun theology as unsatisfactory as Harry's. If his mother believes in a beneficent Providence that sometimes brings good out of evil while Harry disbelieves in any realm beyond that of the empirical, Don ultimately posits a universe not only mysterious but also malevolent in the capriciousness of its workings. Don regards his ten-year-old brother Willie as even more victimized by his maleficent power than he is. The only one in the entire family to take any initiative in preserving the house against encroaching floodwaters, Willie is also the only one to die at the hands of the rushing torrent after the house slides down the bank. Significantly, Don describes the river in terms of snake imagery: "I watched the river continue to rise and twist and swirl and fall back in thick earth-colored coils..." (177). Read mythically, the events played out in the book reenact the biblical fall, expulsion from the garden, and deluge. Before the novel opens, Willie lives in a condition akin to a pre-lapsarian state of innocence, uninitiated both in the biological facts of life and in the process of life eventuating in death and decay. When the family is finally cast out of their Eden by the flood, they leave without the dead son, a sacrifice upon the altar of their apathy and inertia. But whereas the biblical deluge destroyed all but the chosen remnant who remained faithful to the Covenant, this flood ironically destroys the innocent — both Willie and, through a freak accident, Ruth's unborn child — and leaves the guilty to ponder whether the Covenant indeed exists any more. Maybe the universe is just a deistic, relentless machine like the one's in Harry's shed, or an absurd world devoid of any perceivable purpose and meaning.

Before suffering the loss of the house and finally of life itself, Willie loses his sense of the wonder and beauty of sex and birth. His sister Ruth perverts Willie's initiation into the mystery of birth as he watches his dog Lady have her pups by naming it "dirty," thus traumatically awakening Willie's knowledge of shame and sin. But if human stupidity accounts for Willie's awareness of selfishness and bitterness, nature herself, which had tried to show him the process of birth undefiled, gently makes him aware of death and decay; for as Willie beholds the seasonal procession he experiences an epiphany: "seeing and understanding and saying to himself the emptying, the widening, the stretching out of space to distance that is cool, to distance that cools and grows cold and is autumn and the death of leaves, and is time and the someday death of man, of any man and every man and even I" (166). To grow to adolescence involves coming to terms not just with one's sexuality but with one's mortality as well. Don finally sees that Willie, though innocent, is "vulnerable" to the same suffering as if he were guilty, and he rails against the injustice of it all.

In the face of a universe where the unmerited suffering of the good appears as gratuitous as Cordelia's suffering in *Lear,* the only value Don can theoretically reassert is man's "spirit," for it is "not the body and the flesh which are eternal, but that eternity is only in something unknown, the form, the soul..." (130). Yet the main embodiment and purveyor of that transcendent spirit — Willie — lies dead. Those totally lacking in that spirit — Dad, Ruth, Harry — and those in whom it is at best only partially operative — Mother, Don — survive. If Dad just permits the destructive force of nature to take its course without putting up any resistance, Ruth actually compounds nature's destructive tendency by twice attempting to abort her unborn child. Seeing no deeper than the potentially harmful effect of the biological process on her physical beauty, Ruth compares herself with Lady, the "bitch full of pups," "swollen" and "ugly" (67).[3] However physically vital, with "her Hollywood body and soul" (31), she is spiritually sterile. With her posture "in a horribly caricatured and incomplete position of prayer" (89) as she tries to abort the baby on the fence that Harry, at Dad's instigation, has wired to electrocute trespassing chickens, Ruth performs a ritual obeisance to the mechanical God; ironically, the unborn child dies when Ruth stumbles down the stairs, pathetically clutching the clothes she desires above all else to save from the flood's destruction.

Ultimately Don can only despair of the essential "spirit of man," which is largely inoperative in the universe of Wetzel's novel; both man himself and the seemingly capricious force that creates only to confound and destroy are guilty. Don can make his separate peace with Ruth only because earlier he could empathically understand "with a sudden clarity how perhaps it was a truly barren place of loneliness that she had come to inhabit. . . . My God, [he] thought, the torment that it might be for Ruth to remember — to remember happiness and to know that it is gone" (129). Ruth's condition of loss is Don's condition as well, so one can readily understand how one reviewer was led to conclude that Wetzel "is really (and perhaps unconsciously) preaching the doctrine of Retreat from Life"[4] — a doctrine that Anderson's John Bosworth had toyed with and found wanting in *Come Marching Home.*

II All Summer Long

In adapting Wetzel's *A Wreath and a Curse* for the stage, Anderson made several alterations: some, such as not showing the house sliding down the bank into the river, were dictated solely by the exigencies of the dramatic form; others, such as altering events to reduce exposition and to dramatize confrontations rather than just report them, reveal more about Anderson as a playwright. The story remains essentially the same in *All Summer Long* as in Wetzel's leisurely paced novel, the central changes occurring at the end of the play, not only as concessions to the Broadway audience but also as indications of Anderson's different philosophical outlook; Willie does not die, and so far as the audience knows, Ruth's baby will not be stillborn. Anderson compresses the time span as well; whereas the novel's action moves from late spring through late November, providing an autumnal and wintry mood that reflects Wetzel's somber theme, the dramatization ends with Willie's return to school at the end of the summer, which is appropriate to the more optimistic tone of beginning anew and building on what is left — a tone at odds with the book's conclusion.

More substantive than differences in the story line, however, are those in the characters' motivations. Instead of being injured jumping to safety from a burning college boarding house as in the novel, Don is crippled in an accident while driving the faultily maintained family automobile, so Mother can blame Dad. He, in turn, can single her out as responsible for keeping them tied to the house rather than moving away when opportunities for promotions came along, because in the play they live in her grandmother's home rather than on what remains of his father's farm. In general, the relationships between family members in the drama are more strained than in the book, since Anderson pursues more intently his themes of the death of love in marriage and the conflicts and lack of communication between father and sons, both situations that recur often in his later plays. To this end, Anderson increases Willie's age from ten to almost twelve to render the concern over sex education more pressing and heightens as well the close bond between Mother and Don, while Dad, though given a more dominant role, is portrayed much less sympathetically. If Dad's part increases, Harry's diminishes to the point where he becomes the least developed character. Since in the novel Harry serves mostly as a foil on the philosophical level to Mother and Don, he is less useful to Anderson, who must avoid extended intellectual debate and who generally scants metaphysical concerns anyway (so much so that his dramatic version finally has less resonance than Wetzel's book).

Lastly, there is the matter of dialogue, much of which Anderson transfers virtually verbatim from novel to stage. For example, one of Don's long speeches in the novel, replete with biblical phraseology and running to almost one hundred words in the book, reads in part: "I knew and Willie knew and possibly Mother knew that the day would come when the river would have to be reckoned with . . . even if our backs were turned upon it, even if we tried in our various ways to ignore it, to concentrate on books or chickens or Gods or motors or just being beautiful, we still would feel the trembling of the earth beneath us and be afraid" (50–51). In the play, it is given more colloquial rhythms and is altered by condensation so that the entire speech reads: "But you remember, that no matter how we try in our different ways to ignore it, to bury our heads in books, or chickens, or Gods or motors, or just being beautiful, when the time comes and the river rises, we will feel the ground tremble beneath us and we will be afraid" (127).[5]

While the play is still poetic in tone as Wetzel's novel is, Anderson writes less imagistically; instead of verbal symbols, he creates, as is proper to the dramatic form, symbolic props that do not appear in the book — such as the afghan that Willie and Don knit together, which parallels their building of the stone wall that the audience in the theater only hears about but cannot see. The inclusion of such stage symbols adds visual interest, as well as the poetic tone that Wetzel had achieved with symbolic language in narrative passages largely absent from the adaptation.

Anderson's single most important decision in treating the material dramatically rather than novelistically was to discard Don's function as narrator. Even though Wetzel's first person narrative would have lent itself easily and logically to dramatization, Anderson never considered doing this; in retrospect, he observed in an interview in 1974 that utilizing a stage narrator (as he would finally do in *I Never Sang for My Father*) would have demanded a technical expertise beyond his capacity at that point in his development. Yet by not employing a narrator in *All Summer Long,* Anderson sacrifices some of the focus and unity achieved by filtering everything through the consciousness of what Henry James called "the central intelligence." Thus the resulting drama, however much it marks an advance in depth of characterization over the apprentice plays — especially *Come Marching Home* and *Love Revisited* — suffers from a diffuseness in plotting and also from a diminution in force when compared to Wetzel's original. Not that Anderson failed to comprehend the problem; writing with hindsight, he showed his awareness that in *All Summer Long* he was tackling a play structurally different from those that preceded it, a drama essentially of mood rather than of action. "There being little plot or story to carry the play along," he commented after the production, "every moment had to carry its own reward. There being little story, there had to be pattern." He continues, "The patterns develop, just a thread here and a thread there in the beginning, but finally working together into a whole."[6] Whether the play ever attains the measure of unity Anderson ascribes to it is highly questionable.

That several reviewers of the initial production could not determine whom the playwright intended as the focal character — a confusion that would have been alleviated if Anderson had retained the novel's point of view and original ending — is indicative of the problem, though a play need not, of course, focus on one central protagonist, as witness Maggie, Brick, and Big Daddy in Williams's

Cat on a Hot Tin Roof. In his first comment on the play, Tom Donnelly expressed the view that Anderson "has not really succeeded in the difficult job of making a ten year old boy the protagonist of the drama. The older brother is obliged to act as a kind of Greek chorus"; a year and a half later, Donnelly writes somewhat more emphatically, "Willie is nominally the central figure in this play, but he is forever hovering about on the edges of the action," while Jay Carmody insists that "The older brother role . . . is in many respects the dominant one in the new Anderson play."[7] But it was possible — particularly for those who placed *All Summer Long* in the tradition of the "rites of passage" play exemplified so poignantly just a few seasons earlier by Carson McCullers's own adaptation of her novella, *Member of the Wedding* — to regard Willie as the center of the play, since quantitatively so many more of the incidents directly affect his maturation process than they do Don's.

Willie's teacher counsels the family that this summer when he turns twelve will be a significant though difficult time for him, so that even she must have noticed that Willie was not receiving needed guidance at a vulnerable period. His naivete and embarrassment in coping with his burgeoning sexuality reveal themselves in a funny-sad way: like the young Nan Hilton in *Eden Rose,* he sculptures a flat-chested soap carving of the Venus de Milo; and although he plays house in the loft with Therese from next door, he is mystified by her demonstration of breast feeding when she "nurses" her doll. Willie is unlikely, however, to receive any frank yet loving sex instruction from his father. Dad makes no effort to communicate anything except his dissatisfaction with Willie, even terming the elaborate, albeit unnecessarily complicated, cigarette lighter the boy invents a piece of "junk." The younger son fails to fit the mold of what his father wants him to be, particularly now that Don's accident, for which Dad must feel some guilt, has nullified his aspirations for the older boy. No "whiz at figures" (18) like his bookkeeper father and not talented in athletics like his brother, Willie dabbles instead in art and writing poetry and knitting — all associations that Dad, like so many of Anderson's males who subscribe to a faulty notion of what constitutes manliness, objects to. Willie obviously feels insecure around his father, so "afraid" of displeasing him and of being reprimanded for it that he runs away at his approach; and instead of using Willie's need to be taught the facts of life as an opportunity to establish a long overdue relationship of trust, Dad delegates this responsibility to Mother (as Anderson's own father had done). Before she can or does do anything to relieve Willie's ignorance and uncertainty, at Don's prompting he discovers things for himself. That Anderson takes such a prosaic and normally unliterary subject as the need for proper sex education in the home and makes it an important motif here, and again in *I'll Be Home for Christmas,* as well as making it at least a subtheme in several other works, such as *Eden Rose* and *Tea and Sympathy,* is one reason why, as was mentioned earlier, a distinguished academic critic like Robert Brustein likens Anderson's plays to psychological counseling.

Willie receives his instruction in sex from watching his dog Lady give birth to her pups, standing "in wonder and awe at the thing he has seen" (101). But Willie's sister Ruth names what he has just witnessed a "dirty, filthy thing .... disgusting" (107), thereby instilling a distorted attitude toward sex and birth that might never be eradicated. As in Wetzel's novel, this comprises Willie's fall from grace, "the end of Willie as a boy — the end of innocence — the beginning of shame" (113). The only thing that might counteract the detriment done by Ruth's reprimand would be examples within the family of adult relationships built on love and the open display of affection. But these are not forthcoming.

Ruth and Harry argue constantly, showing Willie the tensions underlying an essentially selfish relationship. Ruth saw marriage as her means of escape from the house, yet Harry finds living with her family a convenient and inexpensive way to indulge his passion for cars. Feeling even more trapped than before, Ruth resents Harry; movie magazines, replete with advertisements for cream bust developers and entry blanks for the Mrs. America contest, provide her with an easy entrance into a Hollywood dreamworld peopled by sex goddesses. Barren of inner resources, she is sustained by the movie magazines that Don labels a kind of "dope" in a way that radio soap operas sustain another lonely, disillusioned woman, Lola in William Inge's *Come Back, Little Sheba.* The neurotic Ruth pathetically flaunts her own body (Willie innocently even imitates her suggestive walk), while at the same time acting prudish about sex; as Don points out, "The sexiest girl in the neighborhood, and you're ashamed of sex" (113). She regards her body as an object to be admired and made love to in a mirror; in Act Two, Scene Three, Don comes upon her alone "in the kitchen .... dancing with herself — just sort of swaying to the music of her portable radio — dancing as she can never dance with a man — a sort of pure narcissism" (112). Seeing no value in herself except as a sex object, she feels insecure with Harry, certain that once pregnancy makes her "ugly," like Willie's dog, Harry will no longer love her. In her warped system of values, physical beauty is the panacea for all life's miseries: "All my life, I've wanted only one thing — to be beautiful. I knew if I was beautiful, I'd be loved, and if I was loved I could stand living in this no place, in all this ugliness — and now I'm ugly too" (59).

Since Ruth attempts to destroy the baby on the fence Harry has rigged to electrocute the neighbor's scavenger chickens, the reduction of human life to the animal level is implicit. Willie, who respects life in all its forms — for which Dad taunts him with having "a heart like a girl's" (70) — contrasts sharply with Ruth. Anderson juxtaposes for the audience the almost gothic visual image of Willie cradling in his arms the dead chicken Dad shot when the fence failed to work, "his shirt front covered with blood . . . . in the light of the candles" on his twelfth birthday cake (100) with the earlier picture of Ruth lying on the ground, her stomach bloody from a cut on the barbed wire. At the end of the play, Ruth selfishly and frantically scurries around to save the "gaily colored clothes" (185) that mean more to her than life itself from the encroaching floodwaters that are like a biblical judgment on this family, while Willie unselfishly risks his own life to search for a stray puppy, proof that he has not been totally corrupted by the warped value systems he sees around him. On a symbolic level, Ruth's attempt to abort the baby becomes, then, a physical manifestation and consummation of her inner spiritual sterility; as is true of certain characters in Albee's plays — the Young Man in *The American Dream,* the Angel of Death (also a product of Hollywood) in *The Sandbox,* and even Nick until he undergoes his redemptive change in *Who's Afraid of Virginia Woolf?* — the beautiful blond exterior masks a morally vapid interior and unwittingly reveals a society that has somehow gone astray.

If the marriage of Ruth and Harry provides Willie with a negative example, so too does that of his parents. Late in the play, in an effort to raise Dad in his children's estimation and subconsciously to buoy up her own conviction of the love she will never admit is flagging, Mother reads to the three children a letter that the father, like Charles Webster in *Love Revisited,* wrote to her on their wedding day, pledging unfailing love: "'Well, I'm not just writing this note to tell you I love you. So don't be scared. As long as we love each other, we have nothing to be afraid of. And I'll love you forever and ever and ever'" (123). Yet Willy sadly cannot remember ever having seen any open display of love, even a kiss, between his parents, whereas the less inhibited and emotionally healthier parents of his friend Therese "are all the time laughing together — and kissing. It looks like they're having fun" (46). Constrained because of the stereotyped notion that manliness means never openly expressing one's emotions, Dad has never been able to demonstrate his love; and that inability has perhaps contributed to the decline in that love over the years.

Whether it has been gradual or abrupt, the erosion of the parents' love, like that "of time and the river" on the house, is complete. When Mother and Dad are alone, they wrangle perpetually, much of the arguing overheard by Willie through the bedroom walls with a predictably traumatic effect, for his father often verbalizes his deep-seated belief that they "oughtn't to have had Willie" (52). Willie even comes to wonder, "Why didn't Mom and Dad stop me?" (92). So Ruth's unborn baby is not the only unwanted child in the play. Don, ten years older than Willie, is his mother's "favorite"; she confesses that she has permitted the bond between herself and her first son to become a substitute for the lack of affection between herself and her husband. As the archetypal mother, she sees her only identity as flowing from living for and in and through her children; the home she creates thus provides a "shelter from the world's injury, the world's terror, doubt and division" (33), becoming a womb that protects and isolates its inhabitants.

Anderson, perhaps seeing this as another opportunity to "sing" for his own mother, limns the mother in *All Summer Long* with more affection than Wetzel has done in the book. Whereas there the mother's well-intentioned reliance on a beneficent Providence is not only thrown into doubt but emphatically disproved by events, here the mother's faith tempered with suffering becomes the basis — despite their previous uncertainties — of Willie's and Don's incentive to persevere even in the face of overpowering odds: "You can rise above things with the spirit — I've done that" (51). Anderson's decision to make the mother his raissoneur, a role Don fulfills in the novel, seems an unwise strategy dramaturgically, since the audience might be tempted to dismiss the philosophy of so passive a character and to focus instead on the never quite disguised underlying theme of the futility of the human condition that remains as a holdover from Wetzel's original, despite Anderson's efforts to wrench from the material an essentially hopeful message.

Jo Mielziner, who designed the stage setting and lighting, evidently perceived the play's dark undercurrent and chose accordingly to heighten that mood. Though less elaborate in design and less intricate and poetic in its workings than Mielziner's famous design for Arthur Miller's *Death of a Salesman,* his set for *All Summer Long,* with its skeletal, framework house lacking any real walls and the illusion of the river created solely by "water ripples appear[ing] on the scrim" (3) shares certain affinities with the earlier design. During the pre-Broadway tryout in Washington, Richard Coe faulted Mielziner for creating an atmosphere at odds with the playwright's intention: "Jo Mielziner's eye-catching setting I found disappointing in that it is more Mielziner than Anderson, its muted coloring and ghostly aspect at odds with the positive, youthful vigor of the words, suggesting, if you will a sort of 'Death of a Country Boy,' whereas his rebirth is the play's essential achievement."[8] Anderson must have concurred, for he saw to it that at subsequent performances "the tone of the set [was] very much brighter."[9] But just how much brighter is debatable, for after the New York opening, Brooks Atkinson, who considered *All Summer Long* basically "a negative play" in its outlook, thought that Mielziner had intuited the thrust of the drama and achieved "a memorable set that conveys the dour mood."[10]

Some of that "dour" side springs from the essentially negative characterization of the father, whose role Anderson enlarged from what it was in the novel with the purpose of presenting him as more fallible and judging him more harshly. Dad's failure to fulfill his duties as a father is symptomatic of a general apathy and inertia. In his petty, vindictive way, he conceives elaborate schemes to protect the vegetable garden from the neighbors' chickens, while he does nothing to save the house — as if striking back at it, and indirectly at his wife, for his middle-aged disillusionment over what little he has accomplished. Yet when anyone suggests he is remiss in his duties, he takes the defensive, resenting, for instance, Don's intrusion in the rearing of Willie: "A boy that age doesn't turn against his parents unless someone shows him. . . . Leave him alone, do you hear? He's our son, not yours" (110–11). In effect, Willie has not so much turned against his father as turned toward his older brother to fill a void. In the play's closing moments, all Dad's disappointments over his shattered dreams for his son, all his fears that the paralyzed son will become a burden to him, and all his repressed guilt at his culpability in the accident well up in him, finding expression in a dramatic gesture rather than words as he "begrudgingly hands the crutches" to his now "helpless" son (130), whose physical paralysis is symbolic of the moral paralysis of the family.

Many of the sarcastic barbs that Dad, Ruth, and Harry direct at Don are, though admittedly cruel, justified given Don's self-pitying response to his condition; and, if they hurt individually, cumulatively they nevertheless exert a needed pressure on him. As even his mother charges, Don is hardly less apathetic than Dad, cancelling his plans to return to college after succumbing to a defeatist attitude and "becom[ing] so bitter, so critical" (50), his will to go on completely devastated. He questions despairingly, "What's the use? For what? For whom?" (51). Such cynicism — which John Bosworth in *Come Marching Home* successfully overcomes — is not only self-destructive, reducing Don to a state of ennui and dependence, but destructive of his relationship with others as well. He lashes out at everyone except Willie, largely as an outlet for his self-disgust; Willie is exempt from these outbursts because, as Ruth accurately perceives, Don needs him "believing that you're God Almighty on a throne" (115). Willie, replacing the once cheering fans, does idolize Don; in turn, Don's protective attitude toward Willie — more like that of father to son than brother to brother — reflects his tendency to consider his younger brother as a surrogate for the child he thinks he has no chance of ever fathering. The criticism that hits hardest is Dad's accusation that Don demeans Willie by transforming him into a "male nurse" whose sole purpose is to serve Don at the expense of developing his own interests. Dad's merciless verbal flailing works, and Don soon forbids Willie to perform some of the customary little acts, even if it means groveling in the mud when the crutches fall out from under him.

But Willie continues to assist Don in more substantial ways. Determined to undertake the herculean task of building a raft and then constructing a stone retaining wall rather than stand idly by, Willie restores Don's incentive to act instead of just feel sorry for himself: "At least I can paddle a God-damned raft. If you can build it, I can paddle it, and between the two of us, maybe we can even build a wall" (75). Seeing Willie's capacity to dream and to act decisively to make that vision reality spurs Don on with renewed purpose. As he explains to Willie: "I don't know if you can understand, but a part of me's dead. You plan to grow up whole and strong, and there's nothing you can't do, and then something happens and everything's changed. You've got to — re-orient. That means get your bearings. Figure out some purpose, some reason for doing what you're doing" (93). So Don matures during this summer as much as does Willie, who functions as a catalyst for his older brother.

Anderson's Don, less introspective than Wetzel's — partially because of the difference in genre — finally becomes more positive in his outlook than the character he is modeled on. Don's realization that "if I'd gone down to Harry's shop and worked, I could have earned enough to pay for our wall" (132), implies an acceptance of personal responsibility rather than a holier-than-thou condescension toward others, and it leads directly to his final determination to start earning money so that he and Willie can go to college together someday and Willie can become a doctor. Yet this might prompt a curiously two-edged response from the audience, for not only has Harry earlier described the job in his shop in a demeaning manner, but Don's motivation still smacks of living vicariously through his younger brother. So at the play's end, questions over Don's psychological and emotional health remain, along with the suspicion that he promises to act primarily to reassure Willie that the summer's effort has not been futile, that Willie's example has exerted a regenerative influence and is thus to be valued in spite of their inability to save the house. In short, that this is Don's feeble attempt to ward off the void, and thus akin to Sonya's "We shall work" at the conclusion of Chekhov's *Uncle Vanya.*

For Don realizes that Willie teeters on the edge of "despair" and desperately needs to believe, in the face of all evidence to the contrary, that "no matter how futile it [building the wall] was, it was something — something to face the facts" (129) and "the most important thing you did in your life" (137). The only material remains of all their effort, however, is the afghan that Don and Willie knit together, a visual reminder that not all has been lost, that something endures. Though Anderson might have believed, along with Richard Coe, that he was writing about "rebirth" or the beginning of a renewed life, about creation rather than destruction, the play concludes on an ambiguous note at best, for the spiritual growth of these two brothers, particularly of Willie, remains very much in question.

In his two reviews of *All Summer Long,* Atkinson called Anderson's dramatization "a poignant play" and "a tender and beautiful work of art" in the manner of "a Chekovian portrait." He did, nevertheless, find several things to criticize: an "unresolved and nebulous" quality about the central theme deriving from the fact that "every character is a separate theme"; a lack of a "clarifying point of view" stemming from "Anderson's method of saying nothing in his own right as author [which] leaves the symbolism vague and vapory"; and a plot that "seems desultory and sometimes aimless and general."[11] Certainly the Chekovian influence, virtually nonexistent in other Anderson plays, is strong in *All Summer Long,* not only because this is a drama with a plot so leisurely on the surface as to almost lull the audience into not recognizing that, in Chekhov's words, these people's "lives are being smashed up," but also because it is primarily a mood piece — the swan song of a family so overcome by inertia and petty bickering as to be blinded to the reality that life is disintegrating around them. (At the same time, however, it should be noticed that *All Summer Long* is totally devoid of ironic Chekhovian comedy.)

The symbolism and themes, while perhaps conveyed with a subtlety that places added demands on an audience's attention in the theater, are not, contrary to Atkinson's conclusions, really vague at all; in fact, at almost every point the symbolism underpins the central theme of creation and destruction — both nature's and man's. Nature, like man himself, can be a power for both good and evil (the river), and can work either creatively (the baby) or destructively (the flood). And man can either cooperate with nature in its creation and destruction or choose to defy it in either a positive (overcome paralysis, build a wall) or a negative (kill chickens, abort a baby) way. So, too, men's relationships with one another may be creative and loving (the interaction of Don and Willie) or destructive and selfish (Ruth and Harry, the quiet desperation of Mother and Dad). Man can act or be lethargic; he can accept responsibility or ignore it; he can build up or tear down. In *All Summer Long,* the balance tips in the direction of destruction over creation, making it in both philosophy and tone the darkest of all Anderson's plays.

III *The Genesis of* Tea and Sympathy

Nine months after the Washington premiere of *All Summer Long,* Anderson's *Tea and Sympathy* opened to almost uniformly enthusiastic New York notices and settled in for the second longest run in the dramatist's career — 712 performances. Looking back on the drama a few years later, W. David Sievers called it the "most mature and important play of the 1953–54 season."[12] Brooks Atkinson hailed both *All Summer Long* and *Tea and Sympathy* as "work[s] of art," yet he perceived the essential difference in style and scope between the two, writing: "*All Summer Long* is to *Tea and Sympathy* as a tone poem is to a symphony."[13] Excellent as he found the Chekovian *All Summer Long,* it apparently lacked for him, as it does for most audiences, the size and impact of the more Ibsenite *Tea and Sympathy,* which he later termed "a fully-wrought drama that can stand on its own feet as literature and theatre."[14] Several motifs from the "tone poem" reverberate and expand in the "symphony": the dissection of the father-son relationship; the conflict between husband and wife; the examination of what constitutes true manliness; the sexual education and here as well physical initiation of the young man by the older woman. In relating the two, one could also say that Laura Reynolds is to Tom Lee in *Sympathy* what Don is to Willie in *Summer,* for here Anderson substitutes the relationship between the older woman and the younger man — that reflects his own marriage and that he had earlier explored in *Eden Rose* — for that between older and younger brothers.

Critics looking at *Tea and Sympathy* have discerned similarities between it and G. B. Shaw's *Candida,* Mordaunt Shairp's *The Green Bay Tree,* Terence Rattigan's *The Winslow Boy,* Lillian Hellman's *The Children's Hour,* and Calder Willingham's *End as a Man.* Yet if there is one play that it resembles — and that Anderson must have had at least subconsciously in mind when he wrote it — it is John Van Druten's *Young Woodley* (1925), a drama Anderson readily admits to knowing and admiring.[15] Both occur in private boarding schools (Van Druten's in one at Mallowhurst, England; Anderson's in a New England one clearly modeled after Exeter, which he attended), and both involve a triangle between a brash, athletic, condescending, and sanctimonious housemaster, his younger, lovely, gentle, and compassionate wife — both named Laura — and a lonely, sensitive, introspective, long-haired adolescent, in each case fond of flowers and given to writing poetry.

In Van Druten's play, the housemaster Simmons, already embarked on a purity campaign to rid the house of what he considers an unhealthy aura of brooding sexuality, singles out Roger Woodley, an admirer of Swinburne's overripe love poetry, as the special target for his attack. He comes upon his wife Laura, who understands the emotional turmoil and confusion that besets these adolescent boys, locked in Roger's arms on her birthday and threatens to have him expelled. Roger doubts Laura could ever really have loved a man like the insensitive Simmons, but when she tells him "I was sorry for you. . . . It means no more than that" (41),[16] he feels rejected, destroys his poems, and flees to the arms of a young shopgirl; but that only makes him "feel dirty all over" and "hate [him]self" (47). To protect Laura from the vicious slurs of Vining, one of the other boys, Roger goes at him with a knife. Woodley, Sr., who pleads the gap that he thinks must always exist between father and son as an excuse for "never [having] been very intimate" with him, is summoned, and they eventually go off "arm in arm," but not before Laura convinces Roger that she "still care[s]" for him (60). Earlier she has told her husband, in lines that Anderson's Laura will echo, that the boys "need a little sympathy and understanding. That they can't get from men and from each other. You see them distorted, twisted. You have no feeling for them, save their respect for you" (26). Now she tells Roger, in lines tonally like those of her later namesake, "I want you to treasure the memory, if you can, as I shall — always. . . . don't let me spoil love for you. It's the most precious thing in the world . . . but it is so often wasted and it can be so cruel, it can turn so easily to hate and beastliness. . . . I have loved you, Roger — with all my heart. I want you to know that and remember it, that's all" (60).

Yet if *Young Woodley* exerted a major influence on the plot, characterization, and theme of *Tea and Sympathy* — so much so that it might appear that Anderson was adapting and updating the play for American audiences — there are three works by Anderson himself (a short story, a novel, and an early draft of the play) that coalesce with his memory of *Young Woodley* and culminate in the final version of *Tea and Sympathy* that Broadway audiences saw in 1953. In his unpublished autobiographical short story, "Katherine and Pity and Love and I" (1947), the sixteen year old narrator falls in love with Katherine when he thinks that her marriage to a forty-ish, virile, athletic man must be loveless and unhappy, only to discover how mistaken he is when he sees the impression of their embracing bodies together in the bed. So the boy, who had cast himself in the role of "a lover, a man rescuing her," recognizes that he is "just a growing kid with lots to learn about everything."[17] The title of Anderson's story belies his continuing concern with the nature of "pity" and "love," how they diverge from one another in the motive of the giver, and whether they can coexist without destroying a relationship — a concern developed in both *Tea and Sympathy* and *Silent Night, Lonely Night.*

Anderson's unpublished novel *Birthright,* also dating from 1947, centers on a young writer whose sexual sterility is so psychologically traumatic that it causes impotence, leading his wife to divorce him. He finally meets an actress who, by compassionately giving herself to him, in a gesture that prefigures Laura's at the end of *Tea and Sympathy,* helps him regain his manhood.

The notebooks that Anderson kept preparatory to writing *Tea and Sympathy* — and which he later excerpted for the newspaper of his prep school alma mater — reveal that he "worked on [the play] in 1947, 1950, and 1952."[18] As early as the winter of 1945–1946, he evidently had come upon the title for his still nonexistent manuscript while walking in New York City with his wife and one of her former students. As he later tells the story, the student said she was living in a boarding house where the owner offered her girls "tea and sympathy."[19] Not until 1948, however, did he begin a first version of a play using this title. In it, a young war widow and housemother at a boarding school compassionately tries to help one of the students, Tom Lawson, overcome the shyness caused by his clubfoot through teaching him to dance and arranging a date for him, with the disastrous result that the girl mocks his deformity. At the same time, Paul Bennett, a new housemaster made sterile by a war wound, which has caused his wife to have their marriage annulled, arrives at the school. Sobered by his experiences, Paul has retreated into himself, preaching the need for solitariness, certain that all physical love is basically selfish. Tom comes under the tutelage of these opposites: the gentle Katherine and the bitter Paul.

Eventually, Katherine redeems Paul by giving herself to him, and Tom resolves to find a girl to love.

In one crucial passage, Katherine talks about love as a way of escaping from loneliness and solipsism: "In all of us is the need to be understood, buoyed up, to share. If we are to be alone, we are cut off from humanity, isolated. But in love with one person, we are in touch, through him, with the rest of the world."[20] The convergence of one of Anderson's central themes with a recurrent motif in the plays of Tennessee Williams could not be more exact. Williams writes in his preface to *Cat on a Hot Tin Roof,* "We come to each other, gradually, but with love. It is the short reach of my arms that hinders, not the length and multiplicity of theirs. With love and with honesty, the embrace is inevitable."[21] As one of Anderson's notebook entries for 1947 reads: "it is a play about the loneliness of the individual. We are all lonely. Within ourselves we carry our deadly secrets . . . the source of our motivations . . . the resulting actions. No one understands."[22]

IV Tea and Sympathy *on Stage*

Only in the final version of the drama is one further notebook entry fully developed into a dominant thread. Anderson had copied down, as in a commonplace book, some words from Thoreau: "'If a man does not keep pace with his companions, perhaps it is because he hears a different drummer. Let him step to the music which he hears, however measured and far away.'"[23] What does it mean for an individual to be branded as *different?* This — "judgment by prejudice" — is what Anderson would one day call the "most important" subject of his play.[24] He was not unaware, of course, and neither were a number of critics, of the possible applications of his play to the prevailing atmosphere of the witchhunt unleashed by the McCarthy hearings. This aspect is more muted in his drama, however, than in Arthur Miller's *The Crucible,* which had opened nine months earlier.

In *Tea and Sympathy,* Tom Lee, the "very sensitive" yet "very lonely" young man who hears the beat of "a different drummer," celebrates his eighteenth birthday on the day Laura Reynolds lovingly initiates him into the rites of sex. Since the boy had been conceived to cement together his parents' faltering relationship, the eventual breakup of that marriage placed upon Tom a heavy burden that helps explain his shy, self-effacing quality: "I was supposed to hold them together.... That's a terrible thing, you know, to make a flop of the first job you've got in life" (22).[25] He remembers his mother dimly and unfavorably as someone who told him to go outdoors and play instead of bothering her; and life with father after the divorce became a succession of boarding schools in winter, camps in summer, and theaters and concerts with an aunt in between. Without the least concern for what Tom himself wants out of life, his father Herb demands that Tom live in a way that will reflect favorably back on him as parent: "I *want* to be proud of him. My God, that's why I had him in the first place. That's why I took him from his mother when we split up" (61).

This is not an unreasonable desire on Herb's part, except that he unfortunately suffers, to an even more pronounced degree than Dad in *All Summer Long,* from the mania that he can only feel proud if the son fits neatly into a predetermined mold in appearance, interests, and vocation. In short, Tom is expected to fulfill the stereotypical pattern of the manly man to a tee: wear his hair in a crewcut rather than long and exercise to develop his physique; refrain from taking female roles, even leading ones, in plays at the all-boy school, since Herb's fellow alumni might scoff at him; and become anything but the folksinger he wants to be (Tom opens the drama by plaintively singing "The Joys of Love"). Herb, with his out-of-place collegiate clothes betraying in him the rah-rah boy that he has never outgrown, wants to relive and even improve on his life through his son. According to Bill Reynolds, the housemaster and the elder Lee's protegé, Herb "was always the manager of the teams, and he really wanted his son to be there in the center of the picture" (46). Tom is school tennis champion, but that is a source of shame rather than pride, since "he doesn't even play tennis like a regular fellow. No hard drives and cannon-ball serves" (60). Because Tom does not uphold the stereotype of what a man is and does, he is, in Bill's words, "an off-horse" (63). Anderson, in his notebook, labels this kind of pigeonholing "being branded because you have an enthusiasm others cannot share, or one which is not 'he-manly.'"[26] But Herb will force conformity to his own standards on Tom, saying, in words that significantly combine sport and animal metaphors, "He's going to have to learn to run with the other horses" (63), even if this entails acting contrary to his nature or against his moral norms.

Yet Laura understands (and here she is clearly the dramatist's mouthpiece) that "manliness is not all swagger and swearing and mountain climbing" — Bill's avocation — but must include "tenderness, gentleness, consideration" as well (173). These last are qualities that America's male-oriented society has traditionally ascribed to the feminine sensibility and has intimated that men must suppress. Anderson assaults this artificial, culturally imposed cleavage between the masculine and feminine principles, between reason and emotion, aggression and submission, gruffness and kindness, stiff upper lip and open expression of feeling as a warped way of thinking that produces half persons like Herb Lee and Bill Reynolds, who destroy the life of feeling within themselves and suppress its development in others. Bill's destruction of the book of love poems that Tom gives Laura springs not from sexual jealousy, but from jealousy of Tom's consideration and thoughtfulness and sensitivity to Laura's loneliness and thus becomes a symbolic destruction of Tom for what Bill considers to be his lack of masculinity. Tom's existence is a threat to him and his kind. As Anderson says in his working notes, "The men are playing at being men. The boy and woman are the real adults."[27] Herb and Bill, and not Tom, are the adolescents here, ruled by their game psychology that equates surface strength with inner resources of character; their "winning-is-all" attitude reaches its epitome on the American stage in the morally hollow and fraudulent ex-high-school basketball champions and their cancer-ridden coach in Jason Miller's Pulitzer play of twenty years later, *That Championship Season.* As Laura says, "men think you can decide on who is a man, when only a woman can really know," and she knows that "this boy [Tom] is more of a man than you [Bill] are" (173).

On the exterior, Reynolds is a man's man, "large and strong" with a tendency to be "gruff" (39), but his overwhelming aversion towards Tom, caught innocently sunbathing in the nude with Mr. Harris, another of the masters whose sexuality is suspect, flows from recesses deeper than his jealousy. As W. David Sievers and John Gassner have both pointed out, it originates in his own latent homosexuality.[28] Always happier mountain climbing with the boys than in the company of women, Bill remained a bachelor until forty, perhaps afraid to test his manliness in a marriage relationship. But finally, away from the school on sabbatical, with the ribbing of his colleagues and their wives still resonant in his ears, he needs more than the physical prowess and camaraderie of sports to assuage his repressed fears of his lack of masculinity. Laura realizes that, when they met in Italy, "in some vague way [he] cried out," he "needed help," though Bill defensively refuses to admit this, scoffing at what he would consider an unmanly weakness: "*Me* crying out for help" (54). Laura saw her role as not failing Bill in his need. When she asks Bill whether he persecutes Tom for "the thing you fear in yourself," the stage direction states she "has hit close to the truth he has never let himself be conscious of" (175). Because she has seen through his own insecurity and, he must feel, is taunting him for it, their relationship as husband and wife cannot continue. Like all Anderson men, he cannot tolerate receiving pity, which is demeaning to a human being. To the detriment of the drama's artistry, both Herb and Bill are presented in an irredeemably negative light that establishes a too simple, melodramatic disjunction between the wholly good and unmitigated evil. Gerald Weales remarks caustically about "the old-fashioned cowboy-movie division of the world into the good guys and the bad guys" that "makes impossible any serious consideration of moral problems," while Henry Hewes, in a more reasoned assessment, states that Reynolds "elicits, I'm afraid, no sympathy at all. Perhaps this is necessary to give moral cleanliness to the final scene, but it lowers the level of the play by a good notch."[29]

But if Laura can no longer help Bill, she is now in a position to help Tom, who is "always trying in thinly veiled ways to tell her he loves her" (14), by providing some semblance of a home atmosphere and a compassionate ear that listens and understands. As she suspects, Tom is naive beyond his years in matters of sex (though he is intuitively very mature in his understanding of love) because communication with his father, as was the case with Dad and Willie in *All Summer Long,* has been virtually nonexistent. The only time Herb did attempt the obligatory lecture on the facts of life, Tom "got sick to his stomach." The father realizes "That's a terrible effect to have on your boy" (64), though undoubtedly it was his fault for explaining sex devoid of any emphasis on the dimension of human love that Nan Hilton had been careful to stress in her talks with Roger in *Eden Rose.*

After the incident with Harris in the dunes, which only exacerbates the razzing Tom is already accustomed to receiving over his walking "light" and not having a girlfriend and his "chop-chop" way of playing tennis, he begins to question his own masculinity; his self-doubts are increased by his suspicion that his roommate Al and even Laura think him a homosexual. Anderson is emphatic in his attempts to counter the myth that *Tea and Sympathy* has anything at all "to do with homosexuality. It has to do with an unjust charge of homosexuality and what follows such a charge."[30] Deborah Kerr, who played Laura on both stage and screen, supports this contention in a letter to Vincente Minnelli, who directed the film version, in which she suggests that the drama's integrity would not be circumscribed in the least if the word "homosexual" were never even mentioned — as in fact it could not be on screen: "it *really* is a play about the persecution of the individual, and compassion and pity and love of one human being for another in a crisis. And as such can stand alone, I think — without the added problem of homosexuality."[31]

To regain his self-confidence and to prove his manliness to others, Tom allows himself to be goaded into visiting the town prostitute, Ellie Martin, who is never seen by the audience. There is, however, a representative of physical sexuality on stage at the beginning of the play, and again in Act Two, in the person of Lilly Sears, whose husband warns her that she will "get to looking like Ellie Martin" (125). The comic, if slightly pathetic, Lilly — unlike Laura, who appreciates the difficult times the boys face in coming to terms with their sexuality — loves to tease the boys by preying on their sexual curiosity and flirting with them. Like the Nurse in *Romeo and Juliet* with her totally naturalistic outlook on love, Lilly thinks that an adolescent's whole life is consumed with sex and nothing else. She deliberately wears low cut dresses to dances to "drive all the little boys crazy" (124), and, since she is in her late thirties, she is flattered by the boys' attention and by their gossip that has her "in and out of bed with every single master in the school — and some married ones, too" (8). All of this suggests that the physical side of her marriage is somehow deficient, as was Liz Webster's in *Love Revisited,* and makes her, in this instance, not Laura's foil but her parallel.

What ultimately precipitates Tom's visit to Ellie is Laura's rejection of him. When Tom "impulsively" embraces her, kissing her "passionately" (145), she has the opportunity to prevent his going if she is willing to be more than just an interested bystander and hazard a commitment of self greater than merely providing the proverbial dose of "tea and sympathy" — a traditional role for all the housemasters' wives that is symbolized by the silver teapot that the wife of the headmaster presents to each of them. Laura, instead, recoils from this giving of self and rejects Tom's cry for help. With her protests of "No, Tom . . . No" when he "would kiss her again" (145) ringing in his ears, he sees no avenue left except to turn to Ellie. Anderson's movement of characters at this climactic moment in the play demonstrates his command of conveying a character's internal struggle through mime rather than words. As Tom runs from the housemaster's study and is halfway up the stairs to his room, the troupe of mountain climbing enthusiasts returns unexpectedly; Laura, her mind on things other than Bill's small talk, hides the raincoat Tom left behind while Bill is out of sight, and then closes the door to the hall, hoping to hear Tom's footsteps returning upstairs. But Tom, interpreting the closing of the door as a final rejection, leaves the house, slamming the door; then "Laura turns away from the study door in despair" and sees that Bill "has settled down in the chair intended for Tom . . . . his outstretched hand" before her (148). As Eric Bentley says of the visual impact of the play in general, the "simultaneous action in three playing areas is beautifully counterpointed."[32]

Later, Laura comprehends that the social and ethical strictures that prompted her to say "No" despite the inclination of her heart are wrong and caused her to fail another in time of crisis: "I shock myself. . . . I am responsible here. I know what I should have done. . . . My heart cried out for this boy in his misery . . . a misery imposed by my husband. And I wanted to help him as one human being to another . . . . At the last moment, I sent him away" (171). This pattern of a person withholding compassion from another and then experiencing guilt is a favorite pattern of Tennessee Williams as well. Perhaps Elia Kazan, who directed the play, was able to penetrate to the core of *Tea and Sympathy* so easily because of having earlier directed *A Streetcar Named Desire,* in which Blanche DuBois suffers deep pangs of remorse and regret every time she hears the strains of the "Varsouviana," which recall her rejection of her young husband when she discovered his homosexuality. Afterwards, Blanche needs reassurance of the possibility of forgiveness and of her own ability to love, but when Mitch — with whom she felt "Sometimes — there's God — so quickly!"[33] — discovers her sordid past, he repeats the pattern by rejecting her.

Laura, though a psychologically healthier and sexually more balanced woman than Blanche, still experiences similar misgivings after not responding to Tom, even though to have done so would have demanded a relaxing of her traditional moral code to accommodate what she would ordinarily condemn as immoral, but which, in the situation, would have been the more ethical course of action. So Laura now fails Tom, just as she earlier failed Bill, but for different reasons; however, the second failure is one for which she is morally culpable. Anderson will propound this problem in situational ethics again in *Silent Night, Lonely Night,* his next play.

If Tom is attracted to Laura first as a kind of mother substitute, what attracts Laura to him is his resemblance to her previous husband, John, who was Tom's age when they married. Indeed, their personalities — "kind and gentle and lonely" (134) — and fortunes almost exactly parallel one another. When Laura enters their lives, both are going through the "heartbreaking time" between adolescence and adulthood (53). While in the Army, John experienced some unspecified trial similar to what Tom now undergoes: "He was killed being conspicuously brave. . . . something had happened in training camp . . . . and he was afraid the others thought him a coward . . . He showed them he wasn't. . . . What was it worth if it killed him?" (134–35). Evidently failing to see the application to himself, Tom rushes off to Ellie, with whom he hopes to be conspicuously a man. Failing that, he attempts suicide.

Before Herb hears the full story and thinking only that his son has now proven beyond a shadow of a doubt that he is a "regular fellow," he can finally feel proud of Tom, since both their reputations have been saved, even if it means expulsion for his son. His concern is first for himself and not for the assuredly detrimental effect on Tom. Bill, following the elder Lee's example, takes Tom's failure with Ellie as proof positive of what he has suspected — and what he even hoped would be true all along — that Tom is a homosexual. Bill taunts Tom to his face: "You couldn't be *with* her. Do you understand what I mean?" (154). Feeling deserted on all sides, Tom acquiesces in the judgment of others: "I'm no man and now I know it" (179).

Recognizing that Tom must feel love before there can be sex, Laura reassures him: "You're more of a man than he [Bill] ever was or will be. And one day you'll meet a girl and it will be right" (181). Faced with Tom's continuing disbelief, Laura gives herself to him sexually and, by this unselfish act, is able to restore his belief in his own manhood. Her action is prophetic of what Maggie does for her husband Brick at the end of *Cat on a Hot Tin Roof,* in lines that Laura might have spoken to Tom: "Oh, you weak, beautiful people who give up with such grace. What you need is someone to take hold of you — gently, with love, and hand your life back to you, like something gold you let go of — and I can!"[34] What Laura does say at the electrifying end of this lovely drama, which Sievers terms "as breathtaking a closing scene as a Broadway play has ever had,"[35] is tinged with pathos and humor: "Years from now . . . when you talk about this . . . and you will . . . be kind" (182) — a line so indelibly traced on its hearers' memories that it has often been affectionately parodied.

Laura's motivation in giving herself to Tom involves more than simply expiating her guilt for earlier rejecting him. It cannot be so easily explained away as Walter Kerr thinks when he argues that "The play would seem to have been built backward from the final scene," with the characters calculated to arrive at that point with no regard for his "sense of probability." He finds it most unlikely for Laura "to have married such a man in the first place," except that "being married to such a man" enables Anderson to "set her own qualities in bold relief," and argues that in the closing scene the playwright is constrained by the fact that "the woman *must* seem generous. (She could very quickly seem otherwise.)"[36] In the play itself, Tom Lee questions Laura's motives, asking whether she responds to his need out of love or just from pity. Her reply, "I'm too selfish a woman to love you just out of pity" (145), implies that she sees the relationship as reciprocal, that she receives as much from Tom as she gives him. Though married, she too, as she reveals to Bill, is a "miserably lonely" person (171), and this inaugurates a recurring motif in Anderson of the loneliness *within* marriage that culminates in his most recent play, *Double Solitaire.*

In the year since their marriage, Laura and Bill have grown apart. Bill accuses her: "You never really loved [me]. Because I was not a boy you could mother" (173) — a charge that perhaps contains some truth, as is clear from Laura's revelatory reply: "I did love you because you needed me" (174). Thus she loved him not so much for what she believed at the time she could give to him and do for him as for the sense of responsibility and feeling of being indispensable that he provided for her. Anderson's women, in his earlier plays, need to be needed; they need to pity their men, which is a failure on their part since pity demeans the receiver and casts the giver as morally superior. (In the later plays, as the female characters get physically older, they fail their men in a different way, by not recognizing the male partners' need for physical sexuality.) The most revealing insight into Laura's character — and an aspect that either intentionally or unintentionally he did not fully dramatize — comes from another of his notebook entries: "Possibly in the end she leaves her husband. But to go alone. Not with the young man. I won't even tell you where I'm going. To her husband: You were a lonely man in Italy. I have a natural weakness for sad and lonely men. No doubt it is something neurotic in me. Pity is strong in me. Perhaps I want to hurt myself by getting attached to the wrong man."[37] Anderson suppresses that negative side of Laura, but it lingers under the surface, making her potentially a richer dramatic creation than most critics of the play find her.

Laura's giving herself to Tom is not a totally altruistic act. It fulfills her need to be needed, but beyond that it satisfies a woman starved for sexual affection. Assessing the quality of her marriage to Bill, Laura says, "we so rarely touch anymore. . . . you seem to hold yourself aloof from me. A tension seems to grow between us . . . when we do touch . . . it's rather a violent thing . . . . no quiet times . . . . it's long separations and then this almost brutal coming together" (112). Having always equated gentleness with a lack of manliness, Bill must even make love in a sadistic manner, as if aggressive behavior were another way of proving himself a "regular fellow." Forced into a marriage he did not really want, the sex act has become a vindictive striking out against Laura, and the marriage bed, like the sports arena, a proving ground for virility. Bill thus becomes a third man Laura loved who, "in trying to prove himself a man, showed himself a boy."

Even before giving herself to Tom, Laura has decided to leave Bill; and were it not for an earlier allusion to Shaw's *Candida* (a play for which Anderson has a particular fondness since his first wife Phyllis was older than he) that few probably remember by the final curtain, Laura's action in leaving might be unqualifiedly applauded. Tom is reading Shaw's play and asks Laura whether she believes Candida "did right to send Marchbanks away," to which she responds: "Well, Shaw made it seem right. Don't you think?" (20). Candida's action, sending away the young poet to remain with her husband, contrasts with Laura's. But however "right" Laura's walking out on Bill might "seem" to an audience caught in rapt attention by the play's final moments, it may well have bothered Anderson, deep down, that this woman so full of moral sensibility and compassion could break so cleanly and completely, with no sign of any qualms over the consequences of her decision on Bill. For it is this moral dilemma that he pursues in writing the film version three years later.

V Tea and Sympathy *on the Screen*

Though a neophyte at Hollywood screenwriting, Anderson's years of adapting novels to television for the Theater Guild of the Air provided an apprenticeship for the venture. In transforming his drama into a filmscript, Anderson necessarily made several changes, some dictated by the difference in medium, others demanded by the need to gain approval for the film from the production board. Tame as the treatment of homosexuality in *Tea and Sympathy* appears to today's audiences familiar with a film like Mart Crowley's funny-sad *Boys in the Band, Tea and Sympathy* as written for the stage was too controversial and frank a treatment of the taboo subject for Hollywood in the fifties. Furthermore, Laura had to be served a dose of poetic justice for being unfaithful to Bill; as Murray Schumach indicates, "her adultery with the youth had to be the cause of the breakup of her marriage." He explains also that Anderson denigrates himself for the concessions he made: "'What they made me do for the movies was more immoral than what happened in my play. It is far more immoral that a woman who had not broken with her husband should sleep with this youth than if she had already broken with her husband. . . . You become convinced you're saving the story. But you're not. I will never again give in as I did on *Tea and Sympathy.*'"[38] Yet he perhaps overstates his case, for the screen version, while watered down and weakened in ways that seem patently unnecessary and sometimes ridiculous today, still manages to retain much of its integrity and claim to seriousness, particularly in light of how the censors might have mutilated it. One recalls, for instance, that when Lillian Hellman's *Children's Hour* first reached the screen twenty years before under the title *These Three,* the lesbian relationship had been transformed into a heterosexual *menage à trois.*

The less substantive changes involve "opening up" the play, which inevitably results in a loss of compression through adding the obligatory outdoor scenes; few films, their directors fearing the static and claustrophobic effect that comes from insufficient visual stimulation, are set in only one or two indoor locales like the study and bedroom in the play. So here, in addition, are the Reynolds' kitchen and backyard, the soda shop and Ellie Martin's room, the tennis court, country club, locker room, and beach. The cast, also kept to a minimum on stage, is enlarged for such crowd scenes as Bill and the boys on the Varsity Club outing, or the pajama bonfire, the annual rites of spring when the new boys (Tom, though older, as a transfer student is counted among them) have their pajamas ripped from them (they are wearing shorts underneath) and thrown into the flames; this ordinarily harmless and good-natured camaraderie becomes, for Tom, a sadistic and humiliating experience. Also in the movie, the "big scene" of Tom's visit to Ellie and attempted suicide, only reported in the play, is naturally shown.

Anderson's treatment of the scenes in which Ellie appears demonstrates his film sense, with the visual imagination essential to the dramatist serving him well in writing for the screen, where images must take precedence over words. Erwin Panofsky writes in his essay "Style and Medium in the Motion Pictures," that, in the theater, space — both that on stage and that occupied by the audience — is static or continuous, while in the movies, space — both the locations shown on screen and that occupied by the audience, whose bodies are transformed into a moving camera — is movable or discontinuous. Therefore, if in the theater the audience must choose what it wants to focus on, where it wants its eyes to move, in the film, on the other hand, this choice is made for them by the writer and/or the director.[39] And Anderson usually makes it well. The moviegoer sees Ellie, for example, in only three scenes, but the device of the neon soda shop sign, visible from Tom's window, keeps her in mind even when she is offscreen. Laura, coming face to face with her foil as she does not in the play, finds Ellie less than pretty; the typically Andersonian direction states that "In some vague way Laura wants to reach this girl .... to plead with her ... but all she can do is give her a flower" (88)[40] — one of the special roses she has bought to remind herself of her deceased husband John on what would have been their anniversary. Flowers are always a favorite stage property in Anderson[41] and here hold an increased symbolic importance over the play, where the single flower Tom sends Laura for the dance arrives as an unexpected anniversary present. In the film, one of the first things Tom does is help Laura arrange some cut flowers; and when she mentions "need[ing] some blue in the garden" (6), Tom promises to plant some forget-me-nots. In Ellie's room, the flower Laura has given her serves as a forget-me-not to Tom of the chasm between the loving Laura and the callous Ellie who sells her favors. "Looking directly down at the rose in the drinking glass" triggers "the pain and disgust on his face" (103B) and, together with Ellie's "loud, grotesque laugh," sends him rushing from the room.

More substantial than these changes and additions are the strategies in the adaptation that result from abiding by certain production code standards. Essentially, Anderson takes the play and, by adding a frame at beginning and end, transforms it into a lengthy flashback occurring in Tom's mind. Now married and the author of a novel that retells the story of Laura and himself, Tom returns to prep school for his tenth reunion and settles down in his old room for a long remembrance of things past. By filtering the action through one character's memory, the frame serves, of course, to distance the film audience one more remove from the action than the theater audience had been. Since, however, so much of the story is still seen through Laura's eyes, the framing device results in some inconsistency in point of view; as A. R. Fulton comments, "the scenes in the flash back are not presented introspectively; they are not even consistently presented from the alumnus's point of view."[42] Likewise, some question arises as to why Tom, having already written the novel — a piece of information Anderson suppresses until the end — would recall all this again anyway; perhaps a more sensible framing device would have been to picture Bill Reynolds, on whom the movie focuses at the end, reading Tom's novel. As it stands now, when Tom's memory dissolves on the night Laura offers herself to him, with the poignant curtain line intact, he goes downstairs to see Bill, who gives him a remorseful letter Laura wrote to Tom after reading his book. This coda, that from one point of view might be seen as deepening the moral repercussions, has been harshly criticized by Bosley Crowther as a "preachy postscript" audiences would do well to walk out on.[43]

The frame, though it cannot compare in artistry with the frames of such films as Robert Wiene's *Cabinet of Dr. Caligari* or David Lean's *Brief Encounter,* is, nevertheless, actually less objectionable and deleterious than changes in plot that seriously weaken the characters' motivations. Instead of Tom being seen naked on the dunes with Mr. Harris, the most concrete thing he can be accused of is sitting on the beach chatting with the faculty wives and demonstrating his facility with needle and thread, a skill learned from a succession of maids who tried to substitute for his mother. While this might suggest his effeminacy and exclusion from membership in the tribe of boys, it is hardly adequate, despite the boys' constant razzing, to precipitate doubts about Tom's virility and to lead to his visiting Ellie, with the dialogue all the while getting no franker than the epithet "Sister-Boy." Not even increased emphasis on the ease with which a person's reputation can be smeared makes the audience forgive the flimsy motivation.

Also less candid and couched in innuendo is Laura and Bill's discussion of their inadequate sexual relationship, with her saying little more than that she "gave [Tom] the affection that [Bill] didn't want . . . wouldn't *have*" (113). And Bill's latent homosexuality is never even hinted at, with the result that, as Hollis Alpert writes, "We don't understand what motivates his hounding of the boy."[44] With the real source of anxiety between Laura and Bill presented in so veiled a fashion, it perhaps seems wise that Anderson relegated any discussion of her leaving him until after she gives herself to Tom (which here occurs in a small clearing in the woods), though this change was forced on him by the code. Because of the difference in the causal sequence, however, Laura's guilt over committing adultery and deserting Bill becomes more pronounced, since the blame is wholly hers.

If at the end of the stage play the audience focuses on Laura and Tom to the total exclusion of Bill, in the film version the concluding image is of the lonely man whose life they have all but destroyed, by which Anderson perhaps overredresses the lopsided balance of the drama. In her voice over letter to Tom, Laura has come to the realization that his distorted portrayal of her as "a saint" in his novel is "not the whole or true picture," and that he was much mistaken "about the husband being better off and the wife happy" after she left (123). In fact, the husband is "miserable," lost once again in "the isolation from which Laura rescued him momentarily" (122). Laura, seen here long after the time at which the curtain falls in the play, is now aware of the contradictory moral imperatives, as one expects someone of her feeling and sensibility would be; thus she accuses herself of having chosen the less difficult path of action, of having "answered the easier cry for help" (124), and is almost asking that Tom share the blame. As she is the first to recognize, "We do not live in a glass ball, a vacuum. . . . There are always consequences" (124).

As if Anderson were warning himself that things are never as morally clear-cut as the ending of the drama perhaps suggested, Laura further tells Tom that "a writer has the responsibility of not misleading, of knowing the whole truth as far as he can and telling it" (124). Since Phyllis Anderson's terminal illness intervened between her husband's writing of the stage and screen versions, he might have come to know more of the "truth" by the time he came to write the latter; particularly, he seems to have been in a better position to empathize with Bill's plight as he faces the loneliness of a life without a wife, just as Tom, reading Laura's letter that places an entirely different perspective on their actions from that employed in his novel, gains sympathy for Bill. But Tom's shift is altogether too sudden. Even understanding the external pressures that coerced the change in ending from drama to film — and the internal agony Anderson was undergoing that converged with those pressure — does not erase the aesthetic problem of the film's conclusion. And yet, ironically, the ending of the film — although forced upon him — and not the ending of the play is the one reflected in the conclusions of Anderson's subsequent works up until *Double Solitaire.* So the loss of the dramatist's wife evidently solidified the attitude that marriage must, at all costs, be kept inviolate, which is expressed, at least subconsciously, in the screen version of *Tea and Sympathy.*

CHAPTER 4

Writing for Film

FROM the mid-fifties to the mid-sixties, Anderson was more active as a scriptwriter for films than as a playwright. Beginning with the adaptation of *Tea and Sympathy,* he wrote a half dozen films — four adaptations from other sources and two original ones — while writing only two plays. Anderson, who considers himself primarily a "playwright who occasionally writes movies,"[1] cites two reasons for this shift in emphasis: first, the long terminal illness of his wife Phyllis, which left him too physically and emotionally drained to do much original work; and second, the economics of Broadway, where it sometimes takes years for a completed script to reach production. Given the hit or miss New York theater, where "A playwright can make a killing .... but not a living," he frankly admits penning filmscripts "for money to subsidize his playwriting."[2] But even putting filmwriting in this perspective, he still does not regard it as hackwork. Yet if he has been more fortunate than many novelists and dramatists who have gone to Hollywood in that the directors of the films he has written have always maintained the integrity of his scripts, he understands that the author necessarily relinquishes some of his authority to the director, so that "the theater is preferable for the writer because I simply have more controls over the medium."[3] And, from the literary critic's point of view, writing about drama is equally preferable to analyzing screenplays, since no one has developed a systematic poetics of screenwriting or any tenets for examining a filmscript as an autonomous work of literature divorced from the completed picture.[4] So comments on Anderson's screenplays must necessarily be tentative, focusing primarily on how he has meshed his particular emphases and attitudes with those of the works he is adapting and the modifications that he made in narrative strategies.

I Until They Sail

Anderson completed his filmscript for *Until They Sail,* based on a long short story in James A. Michener's *Return to Paradise* (1951), early in 1957, and the movie, directed by Robert Wise, was released later that year. Michener, who designed his volume so that travel essays on various locations in the Pacific alternate with fiction set in those same places, comments prophetically in "What I Learned" at the end of the book: "Asia must inevitably become more important to the United States than Europe. That is why we must all do what we can to understand Asia."[5]

Both Michener's tale, with its factual epigraph, "New Zealand rushed the cream of her manhood into Africa and Crete; then watched helplessly as Japan crept down the islands,"[6] and Anderson's screenplay focus not on the fighting itself but on the Neville family of Christchurch, especially on the four daughters — Anne, Barbara, Delia, and Evelyn — whose lives become a microcosm of the lives of all women without men during wartime. Whereas Michener narrates the story chronologically, beginning with Captain Harry Neville's return home for Barbara's marriage, Anderson, as in the *Tea and Sympathy* filmscript, tells the story almost entirely through one long flashback in Barbara's mind as she leaves New Zealand for good, pondering whether her father could ever have understood what has happened to his daughters. This changed narrative strategy greatly increases the viewer's suspense, since virtually the first thing one sees is a placard reading: "Jury Retires in Friskett Case" (2)[7] — Friskett being the married name of the younger sister, Delia. Another placard, reading "Shiver [Delia's husband] Not Guilty" (122), signals the end of the flashback and the return to the present.

Anderson discovered in Michener thematic motifs very compatible with his own; both the story and screenplay are about loneliness and the compromising of traditional moral standards that the assuaging of loneliness during wartime often demands. Less importantly, both concern what happens to a civilization that sends its youth off to war, and, even more tangentially, both comment on stereotyped notions of sex roles. In tone, both works display a marked Syngean quality; just as in *Riders to the Sea* it is the men's fate to go out to sea and die there while the women remain at home to mourn their lost husbands and fathers and sons and brothers, so Anne Neville has a premonition that precisely foreshadows a similar fate: "They'll all die in some horrible lost village! . . . one by one they'll be lost. I'm just sick with fear" (16). But while Michener pursues this point, turning it into a philosophical questioning of some dark cosmic purpose by having Anne query, "What is this meaningless business about?"[8] Anderson, who also removes the racial question of intermarriage, avoids focusing on abstract ideological statements in favor of the concrete lives, though he does add a concern over the morality of dropping the bomb. Ultimately, his version is not so bleak as Michener's, even ending (for the Hollywood audience, no doubt) on an upbeat note.

Barbara's flashback, which she undergoes as a way of justifying what the girls have done and had done to them because of the displacement and disorientation accompanying the war, begins with her husband Mark and her brother Christopher (called Kit) going off to fight after their father has been killed and their mother has died. Though the viewers do not see Captain Neville, his influence on his daughters is never forgotten because (much like the portraits that dominate the settings of Ibsen's *Hedda Gabler* and Williams's *Glass Menagerie* and symbolize the lost fathers' values) the home in Christchurch contains the commander's chair, and each of the men who successively sits in it — Delia's husband Phil, Anne's fiancé Captain Richard Bates, Barbara's lover Major Jack Harding, and Evelyn's boyfriends Max Murphy and Tommy — is automatically compared and contrasted with the father. When the men go off to war, the women put straight pins representing the position of each in a large wall map that, together with the radio announcer's voice during news broadcasts, keeps the public side of the war before the audience.

Delia, described as "beautiful and full of fun and tricks" (4), is the first to verbalize the unnaturalness of no contact between the sexes when the men are off at war: "It's the terrible loneliness of Christchurch. . . . All women. It's like suspending life for two years" (20). Without the normal emotional relations between men and women, there will be, she warns, a kind of repression and denial of life: "We're all going to become gossiping old maids and spinsters" (6). She marries the lazy and "disreputable" Phil only because he is one of the few men left behind; once he, too, goes off, Delia leaves for Wellington, where she enters into a series of liaisons with American servicemen "until they sail." Phil is ultimately acquited of killing Delia (a murder that Anderson juxtaposes with their wedding, which, with his fondness for ceremony, he adds to the source) by invoking the double standard that judges men free to do what women cannot.

Contrasted with Delia is her oldest sister Anne, described as "a little prim" (4). Anderson deftly establishes the difference between them in their advice to the fun-loving Kit: Anne admonishes, "I hope he behaves himself," while Delia only wishes "I hope he has a fine time" (6). Shocked at Barbara's tolerant attitude toward Delia and the men in the hotel at Wellington — a location that contrasts symbolically with the family cottage at Christchurch — Anne feels the moral pull between an ethic of happiness and the demands of decency. It is only after she meets, falls in love with, and conceives a child out of wedlock by Bates that she understands Delia's actions, though she is still beset with some qualms of conscience and a fear of rationalizing away her guilt. Anderson supplies this relationship between Anne and Bates with his own distinctive point of view, and it becomes a preview of that between Katherine Johnson and John Sparrow in his next original play, *Silent Night, Lonely Night.* Attracted to Bates because of his Oxford education, Anne, although experiencing the same interior longings he does, rebukes his initial advances, knowing that "a kiss would not be enough for [her]" (55). When Bates, "lonely" and "afraid," "want[s] to kiss" and "touch" her (54), she accuses him of seizing a moment of pleasure with no thought of the consequences, whereas she worries about her reputation and her self-esteem: "I want to be able to still like myself" (55). Very perceptively, she wonders, "Will I be less lonely and afraid if I kiss you. Will you be less lonely and afraid . . . or would it be worse?" (54). Yet after he sails, she experiences regret over holding back, exactly the feeling Katherine Johnson has.

The point at which Anderson's screenplay diverges most from its source is in the characterization of Jack Harding. In Michener, Harding is described as pompous and plump, while Anderson makes him an attractive, slightly bitter man in his late twenties — a literary descendant of Ted Jones in *Eden Rose* and of Paul Bennett in the first version of *Tea and Sympathy* — who has bottled up his heart and hopes to keep it that way through the artificial barrier achieved by drinking. Alcohol becomes a protection from commitment, a substitute for involvement: "I drink and nobody gets hurt. . . . a gentlemanly hangover, but no regrets, and no sense of guilt" (81). Harding is another of Anderson's disillusioned men, like Don in *All Summer Long,* who has become cynical; his first marriage had been founded on nothing other than romance: "she like[d] to kiss in the moonlight and she dance[d] like a breeze and I was never in love before and I never will be again" (90). But after six years of loving her but not liking her, they divorced. When Barbara meets him on a visit to Delia in Wellington (Anderson places their first encounter before Mark's death), Harding is a miserable wretch bound and determined to get himself killed. He shies away from any contact, fearing, like Anne, the moral qualms and guilt, since he has been brought up with sterner standards. Hurt once before, he has withdrawn to the grandstand until Barbara brings him out of his self-pity, breaks down his defenses, and, like Laura in *Tea and Sympathy,* answers his urgent need for help. When Harding must sail, it is Barbara's turn to feel the longing and loneliness, and she goes to him at the end of what Bosley Crowther calls "a bittersweet but basically restrained chronicle" with an "adult approach" that Anderson adapted with honesty and straightforwardness.[9]

II The Nun's Story

Of the three filmscripts that Anderson adapted from sources other than his own works, *The Nun's Story* (1959) results in unquestionably the finest picture, due in large measure to the quality of the original — Kathryn Hulme's rich and haunting book that details the real-life experiences of a Belgian nun who, after seventeen years as a missionary in a nursing order, undergoes a crisis in vocation and leaves the convent. Anderson found Miss Hulme's volume, published in 1956, a "beautiful book,"[10] which is not surprising in that one of the conflicts, that of active involvement in the outside world versus retreat from the world, harks back to his earliest produced play, *Come Marching Home.* Also, its more generalized conflict betwen the opposing imperatives of personal freedom on the one hand and self-effacing commitment to some person (or cause) outside the self on the other was currently in the dramatist's mind, with hints of it occurring in *Silent Night,* also 1959, before it becomes a full-blown theme in *The Days Between, I Never Sang for My Father,* and *Double Solitaire.*

Unlike the adaptation of Michener's short story, wherein Harding is largely Anderson's own creation, the filmscript of *Nun's Story* does not differ substantially from its source. Anderson saw his job as mainly the selection and compression of incidents, with some of the dialogue transcribed verbatim from Miss Hulme's book. What results, as Neil Hurley accurately assesses it, is a motion picture that "play[s the] role of artistic and moral witness in the matter of conscience versus institutional arrangements," intimating that often "tolerance in matters of conscience is less encouraged and more apt to be denied in situations of total institutionalization."[11]

Dr. Van der Mal states the conflict in its bluntest terms very early in the film when he counsels his daughter Gabrielle, just prior to her entry into the convent, "What you're going into is very simply a life against nature" (7).[12] To fulfill the ideal of perfect obedience to the Holy Rule demands total abnegation of self. Gabrielle is given a number in the order (1072) before she is given her name in religion (Sister Luke), and her habit further hides her individual identity; the words "I," "my," and "mine" must be banished from her speech, except in admitting failures in the formulaic "I accuse" (20, 28). She relinquishes her right to talk at will, must detach herself from possessions and even memories of the past, must destroy self-will and replace pride with humility. In short, she must resist anything that would lead to "secularization" (47), becoming, finally, nothing more than "an instrument" at the disposal of her superiors (67). Sister Luke's marriage to Christ is not unlike all those other marriages in Anderson in which the wife is totally subservient to the husband.

Anderson, like Miss Hulme, can understand the ideal of losing self in order to find self and that for a certain type of individual such active passivity might not mean a loss of personhood but, paradoxically, a fulfillment. At the same time, however, the kind of life that Gabrielle enters into involves one denial that Anderson cannot ever be totally sympathetic with: the denial of the need for physical contact between individuals as a natural expression of their shared humanity and as a reprieve from loneliness. When Sister Luke and Simone part, "they want to touch each other in some small way . . . and reach a hand towards the other" (41) — a typically Andersonian line — but, of course, are constrained from doing so. Because the sisters cannot openly concretize their feelings for one another, "true emotion is impossible between them" (119), just as in Anderson's notion of marriage true love would be well nigh impossible without sex. Even the septic quality of the nuns' white habits contrasts with the fecundity of nature, symbolizing that, for Anderson at any rate, there is something sterile about this way of existence.

As her father had warned, Gabrielle has great difficulty in denying self, leading to a constant cycle of self-accusation: "When [she] succeed[s] in obeying the Rule, [she] fall[s] at the same moment, because [she has] pride in succeeding" (38). Her failure threatens to innundate her, as it does Sparrow in *Silent Night,* with destructive guilt and remorse. Upon arrival at her nursing post in the Congo, she becomes the assistant to Doctor Fortunato who, the Mother Superior warns, "is a genius, and a devil. . . . he is also a man, a bachelor, and, I'm afraid, an unbeliever" (79). Sister Luke realizes that, for him, medicine has become a religion, but not in the negative sense that science substituted for religion for Harry in *All Summer Long.* As she says, "I think always he is very close to God in those unearthly hours when he operates" (128). Yet Anderson, who is not ordinarily a metaphysical or religious writer, deemphasizes not only the conflict between science and faith, but also Sister Luke's crisis over why the innocent like Father Vermeuhlen, a victim of leprosy, and Sister Aurelia, killed by one of the natives, must suffer. In so doing, he leaves the audience less ready for the ending.

Dr. Fortunato acts, in a voice over, as a kind of conscience — some would say temptation — to Sister Luke: "You're not in the mould, sister, and you never will be. You're what is called a worldly nun — ideal for the public, ideal for patients. But you see things your own way, and you stick to your own ideas. You'll never be the kind of nun your convent expects you to be" (106). In Miss Hulme's novel, when Sister Luke is to return to Belgium she thinks of "the most difficult severance" from the doctor in a stream of consciousness passage.[13] Since Anderson does not transfer such extended meditations into dialogue, he often demands that the actress (Audrey Hepburn) do through facial expressions what he perhaps should have done through words, and reviewers differ on just how successful she is. While Stanley Kauffman claims complete success for her, writing, "It is her performance — of increasing spirituality and decreasing religiosity — that holds this long picture together," Arthur Knight writes: "Miss Hepburn's face is often a mirror for the unspoken, but it is not quite enough."[14]

Back in "mad," war-torn Europe, Sister Luke violates the order's command not to take sides by working for the underground; her inability to abide neutrality is simply another proof of her inability to be perfectly obedient, her unwillingness to submerge her conscience in something outside herself. When her father is killed doctoring refugees, the crisis comes to a head and she responds with un-Christian anger and condemnation: "I am a hypocrite in the religious life. . . . I wear the cross of Christ above a heart filled with hate. . . . When I think of my father I cannot forgive the enemy. . . . my prayers are arid, and there is only silence between myself and God. . . . try as I would I couldn't regret that an enemy had died" (134–35).

As she returns to the world released from her vows, "the mourning Christ seems to look at her with compassion" (141). The sound of gunfire replaces the sound of cloister bells, just as at the beginning, the sound of the nuns chanting the Divine Office had replaced the Chopin music Gabrielle so loved. And the ring that she had worn as the bride of Christ is now left behind, just as at the start of the film — in one of Anderson's few additions to his source — she had significantly left behind the lover's knot ring that her fiancé Jean (whom she had been forbidden by her father to marry because of insanity in his family) had given her. Harold Toliver's discussion of the way symbols function in film aptly describes Anderson's practice here: "The camera collects items as mute juxtapositions and sequences but not in the quiescent way the stage does. Its objects may intrude forcefully upon our attention by the simple fact that the camera fills the screen with them and for the moment gives us nothing else to see, or centralizes some object for an instant among a flow of other items that await their turn."[15] Leaving habit and ring behind, Sister Luke might return to the world and be in it, but, the audience must certainly feel, she will never be totally *of* it. In that, she is like John Bosworth of *Come Marching Home.*

III A Small Part of a Long Story

With the exception of a filmscript entitled *The Tiger* (which forms the basis for the stage and screen versions of *I Never Sang for My Father*), Anderson has written only one other original screenplay, *A Small Part of a Long Story* (1962), and that remains unproduced, the reason being, Anderson suspects, casting difficulties stemming from its "clinical" nature,[16] for this comedy about marriage recounts in adult and explicit, albeit tasteful, terms the funny-sad story of a young couple's attempts to conceive a child. (England's famous directors of comedies, John and Roy Boulting, managed to make a popular film on this topic in *The Family Way* [1967] and David Rudkin a highly successful play in *Ashes* [1974]; but John Steinbeck encountered the most disastrous reception of his career when he tackled the same subject in the play *Burning Bright* [1950]).

Set during World War II, the actual fighting here remains even more a matter of ambience than it has in *Until They Sail,* present visually in only a few shots, such as that of "the fleet anchorage at Ulithi preparing for Iwo Jima" (75)[17] — where Anderson had written his first "learning play" — and aurally in such period songs as "I'll be Seeing You" and "I'll Be Home for Christmas." Poised against this world at war is the love of Ensign (later Lieutenant) Jeff Bridger, twenty-five, and his twenty-four year old wife Katherine (called Kit), who, at one point, "kiss as though to obliterate the world terror by an intimate, personal act of reassurance" (24). But the separation that war causes exerts a far less deleterious effect on their relationship than does their inability to cement their marriage through children. What they must learn is that marriage can survive and, what is more, be creative, even without offspring. Ironically, yet understandably since Anderson and his first wife Phyllis had no children either,[18] Jeff and Kit's marriage stands among the rare happy ones in all the playwright's works.

Like so many of the author's married men, Jeff regards Kit as the "condition of his life," telling her, "My life didn't begin until I met you" (76). And when they stop taking precautions and try to conceive a child, both of them sense more intensity in their relationship; so sure are they of their success in the endeavor that Jeff celebrates the occasion by giving Kit "gold charm baby shoes" (16). When Kit does not become pregnant, they settle on the home remedy of having sexual relations every night of the month, but this has the unexpected and unwanted side effect of taking love out of sex and dehumanizing it. Anderson sees the comedy in their prescription and conveys the ludicrous reduction visually through Jeff's rushing home at the same time each night, jumping into bed without so much as a kiss, and crossing off the days on a calendar

that once sported an advertisement for baby food but that is finally graced by "a voluptuous girl" (39), this last thoughtfully supplied by Kit as a support for his flagging intensity. Sex has become a frantic endurance contest, in Kit's words, "Kind of like roulette. Cover all the numbers. You can't lose" (27). And Jeff, always the clown, humorously defines himself as "like Pavlov's dog. I have a feeling that for the rest of my life whenever I hear a clock strike seven, I'll get up and head for the nearest bedroom" (40). This verbal animal imagery is reiterated visually when Kit, after Jeff's marathon lovemaking, presents him with "a little ribbon with a medal on it . . . The medal has a small bull on it: For bravery . . . in propagating the human race" (56).

Instruments for measuring the passage of time — calendars and clocks — fittingly become even more important visual symbols, since they indicate that Jeff and Kit live mechanically rather than naturally, forced into a rigid framework of times to have sex, rather than spontaneously making love as an expression of affection. Thus, even though the montage sequences in Anderson's script tend to be marred by bridging shots of the clichéd, Hollywood variety — for example, Jeff's "hand . . . crossing off" days on a calendar (32), or Jeff on board ship reading letters from Kit, "intermingled with kamikaze attacks," while his uniform is successively that of ensign, lieutenant (j.g.), and finally lieutenant (77) — they often convey a meaning along with effecting transitions. In measuring life quantitatively, Jeff and Kit diminish the quality of their marriage.

After first Kit and then Jeff seek out medical opinions, not only does the movie become more serious in tone, but it also unfortunately, if temporarily, takes on the aura of a lecture about the necessity for adequate sex education, a topic Anderson broaches more subtly and in a less documentary fashion in several of his plays. Both of them come to see that their knowledge about the facts of reproduction was no more advanced than euphemistically regarding intercourse as somehow "Like a shot machine" (72). The doctor clues them in on how to determine a woman's peak period of fertility and, through a full screen "microscope view of spermatozoa" (80), lectures Jeff on the subject of "reduced activity of sperm cells" (82) — subjects hardly calculated to be very entertaining, but probably certain to be somewhat embarrassing, to a movie audience.

Such lapses in imaginative conception, along with much maudlin writing, mar what would otherwise be a mature sex comedy, and one that provides a serious look at two of Anderson's recurrent motifs: the difficulty of fusing love with sex, and the potentially destructive stereotype of masculinity rampant in American culture. When Kit believes herself infertile — continuing the animal imagery by referring to herself as "a barren bitch" (43) — she thinks more of what this means to Jeff in terms of depriving him of a child, concluding, "If I can't have children, I shouldn't have married" (59). When Jeff, on the other hand, discovers his sterility, he thinks first of the blow to his virility. From the first he had associated being a father with the notion of manhood: "I guess it's some instinctive sense of completion . . . a man" (14). So the fact that he may never father a child becomes "the theft of his birthright" (86), plunging him into a period of self-pity and despair: "One minute you're a man . . . full and complete, and the next . . . nothing. Hollow. Nothing. . . . I'm sterile. Empty. A shell. . . . I disgust myself . . . all the jokes about the baby. Me a powerhouse. . . . I hate my body. It's a sterile fake . . . I feel dead" (89–90). This is the culmination of an almost obsessive concern in Anderson — begun in the unpublished novel *Birthright* and continued in the first version of *Tea and Sympathy* — to deny that sterility has any necessary connection with impotence, as if he somehow needed to prove to himself that not having children makes one no less a man.

Like Tom after his public humiliation in *Tea and Sympathy,* Jeff needs reassurance about his masculinity; in his feeling of impotence, he even tells Kit, "I feel I could never make love to you again" (92). When the medical treatment he undergoes has no effect, it remains to Kit to give Jeff back his sense of dignity and self-respect, as Laura did for Tom in *Tea and Sympathy.* Dr. Payson (himself coincidentally unable to father children) counsels Jeff to not regard his sterility as the central fact of his life with Kit: "This is only a small part of the very long story of your life together . . . a very small part of a very long story" (106). What Jeff learns — and what a number of other Anderson protagonists have greater difficulty in understanding and accepting — is that there should be no shame if the man is just as vulnerable as the woman, that in a mature relationship the husband need not always be the stronger either physically or emotionally. "Let her love you," Payson tells Jeff. "You feel very unworthy of love at the moment . . . she's loved you all these years for your strength. Now — let her love you for your weakness . . . for the hurt you've suffered'' (106). It remains for Kit to keep that love from degenerating into pity that would demean Jeff even more. If the ending of *Tea and Sympathy* had served as a sort of preview for the conclusion of Williams's *Cat on a Hot Tin Roof,* Kit's closing speeches in *A Small Part of a Long Story* verbally and tonally echo those of Williams's heroine: ''If our having a child will be a miracle, then I insist on a miracle. But first I insist on my husband back with me again as my husband and my lover. . . . I will give you a child. You will give me a child . . . but only through love. The child within me knows that . . . and it is waiting. The miracle is waiting to happen'' (109). What might seem like a facilely optimistic ending is undercut, ever so slightly, by the nagging implications of Jeff and Kit's final gesture before the fade out: ''They hold each other tightly, desperately, their faces wet with tears (109).''

IV The Sand Pebbles

In adapting *The Sand Pebbles* (1966) to the screen, Anderson saw his major problem as ''getting some progression and spine'' into Richard McKenna's discursive novel — in Anderson's words an ''enormous book with no shape''[19] — about the nationalistic movement in China during the late twenties. Despite Arthur Knight's judgment that the finished product is a ''brilliantly succinct script . . . . that keeps hurtling forward for more than three hours with scarcely a let-up in pace,''[20] Anderson realizes that he failed to do the necessary pruning and tightening, as can be inferred from his comments about the finished picture as ''infinitely too long,''[21] and as not fulfilling the dramatist's dictum that each scene must necessarily follow from the preceding one and lead into the next. Robert Wise, the film's director, recognized this difficulty too: ''I think one of the problems, in retrospect, was that we tried to tell too much of Richard McKenna's book.'' Part of the difficulty lies as well in the blockbuster nature of the movie; here is an historical epic whose subjects — foreign involvement in a nationalistic conflict and, secondarily, racial prejudice — dovetail neatly with the ''big'' topics in America during the sixties — the Vietnam War and the Civil Rights Movement. As Wise would later say: ''I was showing that American military might, displayed around the world, had been unpopular for many years, that the phrase 'Yankee go home' was not just something that came out of post–World War II, but had been in existence the whole century. . . . the message of the film was to make that point, that Vietnam should be seen in this historical context."[22] Undoubtedly this ability to see the present in the past accounted in some measure for the popularity of McKenna's rambling bestseller (1962), with its interminable descriptive passages in which sophomoric techniques like italicizing onomatopoetic passages pass for style. Though the film did not fare as well as the book, Hollywood, as if to prove its social awareness, nominated it for best picture.

George Bluestone, in the theoretical introduction to his excellent volume *Novels Into Film: The Metamorphosis of Fiction Into Cinema,* succinctly states what the process of adaptation ideally entails: "What happens, therefore, when the filmist undertakes the adaptation of a novel, given the inevitable mutation, is that he does not convert the novel at all. What he adapts is a kind of paraphrase of the novel — the novel viewed as raw material. He looks not to the organic novel, whose language is inseparable from its theme, but to characters and incidents which have somehow detached themselves from language and, like the heroes of folk legends, have achieved a mythic life of their own."[23] Anderson, however, does little more than "convert" McKenna's novel, for the most part just deleting certain incidents and minor characters. Since his procedure in adapting *Sand Pebbles* is not much different from that in adapting *Nun's Story,* the qualitative difference between the two filmscripts must arise from the superior artistry of the latter source.

Given the change in medium and the difference in prospective audience, Anderson wisely opts for a strictly chronological approach to the narrative. Whereas McKenna's novel opens with Jake Holman arriving for duty on his new ship, the *San Pablo,* and then flashes back to render the immediately preceding events before again moving forward, Anderson begins with the prior events, thus quickly clarifying for the viewers a probably unfamiliar period in Chinese history and introducing the missionary teacher Shirley, who provides the obligatory "love interest" in both novel and film. Anderson deftly handles this exposition and presents as well one of the three prevailing angles of vision on the political conflict through the missionary Mr. Jameson, en route to China Light. Jameson, "the man of peace" (188),[24] stands against the foreign treaty powers, who with their gunboats are, he believes, interfering in what is basically an internal civil struggle that will result in nationhood. A turn the other cheek Christian, he trusts God above guns and will not allow militarism to be confused with mission. His revulsion against "manifest destiny" in all its forms and the divisiveness resulting from colonialism eventually prompt him to renounce citizenship in any state; as he says, "It's too late in the world for flags" (183).

While Jameson understands the political situation well enough to formulate an ideological stance, Holman is, at the beginning, aloof from it, uncommitted even to upholding the position that he theoretically should as a member of the navy. Because of a youthful experience — more hazily sketched in by Anderson than it had been by McKenna — in which he was unjustly punished for an offense actually committed by the son of a town official, he is disdainful of the system of which he is nominally a part; he rebels against being a cog in a well-oiled machine larger than himself and represented by the gunboat's commanding officer Collins. Called by Anderson "the man of war" (188), Collins is the antinomy to Jameson; war *is* his mission, and he undertakes it with a religious fervor.

Jake, in another variation on the freedom-versus-commitment theme seen in *Nun's Story,* rebels against military regimentation and all the overtly theatrical side of it, the patriotic attitudinizing and rah-rah bombast that Collins revels in. To Collins, outward honor is all; when Jake mercifully kills the coolie Pohan whom the native crowd is brutally torturing, in the commander's eyes he contaminates the ship, and Collins must then either purify it or take his own life in disgrace. To regain the lost honor, this commander who is ordinarily a stickler for rules ignores the order to retreat and goes instead to China Light to rescue those who do not wish to be rescued. But Jameson refuses to give meaning to Collins's heroics by leaving. War easily degenerates into a game, just another of the ways, like athletics and sexual performance in *Tea and Sympathy,* that men use to prove their masculinity; as John Sisk notices, "there is a pronounced and game-like element in military life and operations . . . . Armies make so much of sports and games not simply to diffuse potentially dangerous libidinal energies, and not simply because young men like sports and games, but because athletics are important model-situations for the kind of organized all-out effort that armies depend on."[25]

Like the biblical Jacob, the antihero Holman is an isolated wanderer. The men on the *San Pablo* consider him a "Jonah" in their midst, a curse upon them who eventually becomes a much-needed scapegoat. For Jake's surname, one should read "whole man," for that is what he becomes at the end of his epic odyssey toward selfhood. Filled with cynicism, he has cut the ties between himself and others and for seven years been on a journey seeking a home; he thinks that he has found it in the engine room of the ship, but later comes to regard China Light Mission as his utopia. Like the sailors in O'Neill's sea plays, the men on board the gunboat talk of her as a "home" and a "feeder"; and like Yank in *The Hairy Ape,* who finds a meaning for life in the connection that the ship gives him with the sea and the cosmos, Jake senses that meaning through the engine that he can control. Unfortunately, the direction and cinematography fail to capture the essential poetry of the engine in motion. If certain shots in the picture, such as the steaming ship cutting through water and the engine pulsating at full speed, likely remind the viewers of similar shots in Eisenstein's *Battleship Potemkin,* they also suffer by comparison since they lack any symbolic resonance.

Severed from the warmth of a physical home, Jake has also cut himself off from affectionate human contact; until he meets Shirley, he is uncomfortable with any woman except whores who demand no commitment and give no compassion in return. Now the reverse process is at work, as he finds his engine, his friends, his woman, his home. In one of the only two quintessentially Andersonian scenes in the film, we see Jake's hesitancy at being touched by another person. Shirley reaches out to the distressed Jake after he has shot Pohan, but he recoils from what he interprets as pity: "His loneliness is unbearable, but he doesn't know how to accept compassion. . . . She sees his anguish, instinctively reaches out and touches his arm. It is a new experience for him — pity and tenderness from a woman. He looks at her hand with a mixture of longing and fear. She removes it. . . . Holman looks up at her face, a fearful, quick glance. She tries to smile reassuringly at this man who is so reluctant to be reached" (102). Yet the love plot is never adequately developed, and the climactic moment in the film fails to bring together the personal and the public conflicts, since it does not involve Shirley.

The only other scene in the picture that might accurately be called "pure" Anderson is the touchingly simple marriage ceremony involving Jake's sympathetic shipmate, Frenchy Burgoyne, and Maily, the half Oriental–half American girl who provides a handy foil to Jameson. If he consciously chooses to be stateless, she is by birth rather than choice a woman without a country. Like Jake, she is condemned to homelessness; by profession a whore, she is treated by everyone except Frenchy and Jake as an object, just as the men on board the gunboat become tools of the American system.

When Jake dies in front of the still crated machinery at the mission where he intended to stay, his home is ironically snatched from him at the very moment he finds it. Yet he sacrifices his life so that Shirley can reach safety, making the film's ending more positive than that of the novel. Even though *Sand Pebbles* is not the best of Anderson's filmscripts and although only one of his screenplays — *I Never Sang for My Father,* which will be discussed later — can stand up against the best of his dramas, John Gassner's judgment that Anderson is "one of the most intelligent and cultivated of Broadway playwrights, who has also given Hollywood the benefit of his sensibility and skill without disgrace"[26] is essentially sound.

CHAPTER 5

The Marriage Plays

IN response to those who ask why he does not write about something other than marriage, Anderson, denying that he ever feels he is simply "going over old ground" when he begins a new work, remarked recently: "Marriage is often the arena of the plays, but not always the real subject matter."[1] While none of the five plays examined thus far is totally without reference to marriage, in only one — *Love Revisited* — is it, strictly speaking, both "arena" and "subject," for neither in *All Summer Long* nor in *Tea and Sympathy* is the marriage relationship his central focus. But in *Silent Night, Lonely Night* and, especially, *The Days Between* — and later still in three one act plays (*The Footsteps of Doves, I'm Herbert,* and *Double Solitaire*) — Anderson returns to the careful delineation of the relation between the sexes within marriage that, though by no means his exclusive concern, had dominated *Love Revisited* and *Eden Rose* during the apprenticeship period.

I *Anderson and The Playwrights Company*

When Anderson's *Silent Night, Lonely Night* opened on Broadway in 1959, it became his third successive play produced by The Playwrights Company, of which he had been a member since just prior to the opening of their longest running production ever, *Tea and Sympathy;* it was also, with the exception of nonmember Gore Vidal's *The Best Man,* the last of the seventy dramas to open under the auspices of that illustrious company founded over twenty years earlier. Five of America's then leading dramatists, Robert Sherwood, Maxwell Anderson, S. N. Behrman, Sidney Howard, and Elmer Rice — with the exception of Behrman all winners of the Pulitzer Prize for drama — had organized The Playwrights Producing Company in 1938 in rebellion against, and as an alternative to, the domination of the theater by producers who exercised absolute financial and artistic control over their productions, in everything from selecting a director and cast to making changes in the script. The agreement entered into by these five practicing dramatists called for "each author [to] submit all his plays to the Company for production" and granted to "the author . . . the final say in all production matters within the budget."[2]

Writing about his selection for membership, Anderson, who had the signal honor of being the only new playwright ever to be elected to membership after the group's formation, drew upon a term from his navy days, "with but below," to express his awe at now being the close colleague of the very men, Sherwood, Maxwell Anderson, and Rice, whose works he had "read and studied when [he] was in college": "It is not often that a man can mingle with his heroes, much less be of their Company."[3] (Coincidentally, of course, and perhaps confusingly to some, Robert Anderson's name combines the first and last names of two of the group's founding members.) He felt that the distinguishing mark of the company as a producing agent, differentiating it from those producers whose first concern was economic, was that "by and large, it is the body of a man's work that matters, and if he has a play that he wants to write, and it is a good play, usually it is produced, whether or not it looks like a success. The company gambles on the man[,] not on his individual plays."[4] Prophetic words, since, ironically, only one of Anderson's three dramas with the Playwrights Company was a commercial "success."

John Wharton, the company's lawyer and, more recently, chronicler, feels that Anderson, with his background as a teacher of playwriting, came well equipped to "analyze a script as skillfully as any playwright member except Sherwood," and further speculates that Anderson, after Sherwood's death in 1955, might have been able to affect a resurgence of the faltering company had conditions been favorable: "I have not the slightest doubt that Anderson could have relaunched it if there had been available four playwrights of his age, talent, and point of view." But, according to Wharton, the distinctive "point of view" that had been the hallmark of The Playwrights Company's founding fathers — a liberal belief "that people were capable of improvement and that perhaps the greatest feature of that improvement would be a reduction in

Man's inhumanity to Man"[5] — had itself become an unpopular philosophical tenet for a dramatist to espouse after 1950.

II Silent Night, Lonely Night

Although *Solitaire/Double Solitaire* would have a shorter Broadway run, *Silent Night, Lonely Night* actually garnered the least complimentary critical notices of any Anderson play — and not without some justification — though John Gassner, in choosing it as one of the "Best American Plays" of the late fifties and early sixties, termed it "the work of a mature and responsible writer who let his heart and sympathetic intelligence talk out for him under the quiet control of taste and normal tact."[6] The story of this almost actionless, essentially two character play is simple: Katherine Johnson and John Sparrow, both married but each temporarily alone, meet in a New England inn on Christmas Eve, come together out of a mutual need for emotional contact in a long night's discussion of their very similar problems culminating in a one time sexual encounter, and then part, each returning to his or her spouse. Examining as it does the condition of loneliness, as well as the temporary setting aside of traditional moral norms in favor of a higher morality of responding to another person in time of need, *Silent Night* displays thematic affinities with both *Tea and Sympathy* and *Until They Sail.*

To the extent that the greater part of *Silent Night* is taken up in exposition rather than ongoing conflict, it marks a definite decline in Anderson's technique from the plotting of *Tea and Sympathy,* and even from that of *Come Marching Home, Eden Rose,* and *All Summer Long,* wherein Anderson handled the exposition so effortlessly to have it be all but unnoticeable. But here, one is tempted to say, he substitutes exposition for drama, for the "Forward-moving action" that "holds our interest while we are absorbing the richer texture of the characters and the relationships. ... The majority of the plays I read or see which do not 'work' are static. ... brilliant in the observation of human nature, but they start nowhere and get nowhere."[7] So Anderson himself confesses that *Silent Night* "did not work on Broadway," that, despite his intention, he had not prevented it from "seem[ing] to many a static play": "I meant it as a fairly dynamic play in which the 'lives' were only important in so far as they bore on the immediate developing situation between the two people on stage. It is a very subtle difference, but it makes all the difference.''[3] Most critics, however, did not catch the difference. Gerald Weales, for instance, in an extreme statement of a view typically held, finds it ''a relentlessly dull play .... [with] no dramatic material in it at all; it is simply a long double narrative.''[9] No one can deny that much of *Silent Night* is lengthy — albeit literately crafted — confessional speeches in which Katherine and John reveal their pasts, thus inaugurating a perceptible tendency in Anderson to write plays with a form akin either to group encounter sessions (this work, *Double Solitaire,* and, to some extent, *The Days Between*) or to a therapy session (*I Never Sang for My Father*).

Whereas Bill Reynolds in *Tea and Sympathy* felt constrained from crying out audibly for assistance since that would be an admission of unmanly weakness, Katherine Johnson in *Silent Night,* unable any longer to bottle up within herself her need for support or to impose artificial control over herself through the ritualized format of the game of solitaire, actually does utter the plea ''Help!'' — hardly expecting it will be overheard by one of only three other guests in an inn that has plenty of room on Christmas Eve since, as the servingmaid Mae says, ''everyone's got a home is in it'' (4).[10] But Katherine's house in San Francisco is empty of the family who would make it a home: her son Jerry, a student at a boarding school near the hotel, lies confined in the infirmary there, while her husband Dick, often absent on extended business trips, remains in London where, as she knows from a letter conspicuously displayed for the audience on the dresser, he has taken a mistress. They had entered marriage hoping to find an unreal isolation from the outside world, but discovered soon enough, like Liz and Charles Webster in *Love Revisited,* that material concerns impinged on their snug withdrawal; marriage, which brings with it ''the first bills and responsibilities'' (45), can, paradoxically, mean the beginning of the end of love. The same fate will in all probability befall Philip and Janet, the idealistic young honeymoon couple who complete the quartet of guests at the inn. If they provide Katherine with a nostalgic glimpse of the way she and Dick were in their youth, Katherine and John, in turn, thrust the younger couple forward into the future, hinting at what they will become.

Even before marrying Dick, Katherine offered him total dedication, acknowledging that it might necessitate a diminution of her own need for self-expression. She willingly subordinated herself to helping her husband fulfill his drives and ambitions: "We'd promised to love, honor and succeed . . . and he'd succeeded" (39). In Simone de Beauvoir's phrase, Katherine "spontaneously preferred another existence to her own." This ideal of total commitment is an offshoot of the strict moral upbringing she received from her father. He inculcated her with a puritanical, repressive ethical system, symbolized by the "odd pendant" (7) on the key chain she carries with her: "It's the eye of God. . . . It was to remind people that the eye of God was on them" (13) — a symbol Anderson discovered in Kathryn Hulme's *Nun's Story* but did not use in adapting the novel for the screen. John, who as a student had always found his life bounded by "shalt nots," interprets the pendant as "kind of like a neon light blinking, 'No!'," whereas he values the freedom that permits one to experience life without any artificial restraints that inhibit one's development: "they should paste a big label on youth! 'Perishable. Use at once!'" (14). Yet not as strong a conflict as one would expect from such divergent ideologies ever actually ensues.

Twice during her marriage, Katherine has faced and overcome the temptation to ignore what "the eye of God" represents. In the first instance, a seriously ill friend spent "five or six months in the hospital . . . dying" (37) — the first in a long succession of incidents in Anderson's works that allude to the death of his wife Phyllis — and her friend's husband asked Katherine to go to bed with him. Aware only of how this would cheapen her in her own estimation, she refused to assuage his loneliness. Although admitting she has "hated [her]self ever since" for saying no, at the time she felt compelled to honor "a book we live by" (38). For her, moral conduct has always been a cozy set of absolutes that protect her from the difficulty of responding to each separate situation on its own terms: "I'm not strong enough to make up my own rules as I go along. . . . I sometimes wish to God I were" (38). Katherine's values underwent a second scrutinizing in her relationship with a young writer. Unable to communicate openly to Dick the depth of her loneliness even within marriage, she bared her soul in a sequence of poems she subsequently shared with the poet with whom she fell in love; on the verge of succumbing to her passion, she saw the pendant in her purse. This time, since the temptation involved a wholly selfish satisfaction of sexual desire, the "no" against adultery was more emphatic, and was succeeded "not [by] hate," but only by a sense of "Regret, maybe" (40).

John, who "imagine[s] if we could hear all the stifled cries for help in the world, it would be deafening" (34), has always managed to suppress his own urges to cry out with a characteristic tightening of the lips, and yet for a long time has "had the desperate impulse to reach out a lonely hand to touch someone" (35). At forty and venturing into middle age, John experiences "intimations of mortality" (12). Anderson's characters, particularly the males, find themselves vulnerable to attacks of moodiness as middle age — a hardly less traumatic time for them than adolescence, if for different reasons — approaches, for it affords an opportunity for measuring one's accomplishments against one's goals, which is often a source of disillusionment. A more disturbing situation arises if the middle-aged person concurrently undergoes a shift in his value structure, accompanied by uncertainty over whether the rules he has lived by still retain any validity. Instead of easy answers and a comfortable security, a mature person like John, seeking "some certainty," is confronted with "a rage of contradictions ... a saddening but somehow beautiful complexity" (33). Yet if this complexity challenges John rather than dulls him into nonproductive lethargy, he is enough of a realist, without being cynical, to acknowledge the frequent disparity (however unjust it seems) between one's actions and their results; once a believer in a neat system of rewards and punishments, he "Now .... know[s] there is no Prize Day" (43). But instead of buckling under and despairing, he stoically asserts the family motto: "*Dum spiro, spero* .... While I breathe I hope" (16).

One compromise that John made with his ideals was his acquiescence to his family's wishes that he not become a writer; instead, he decided to teach and "write on the side." After the war he did, nevertheless, perform his "duty" and write the obligatory novel, entitled *The Comfort of Your Company* — a title that could easily fit Anderson's play itself. In this drama with few characters and minimal action, Anderson ingeniously employs John's reconstruction of his autobiographical novel as a variation on the double plot. Significantly, the novel's conflict revolves around an incident very similar to the two from Katherine's past: the night before John sailed from San Francisco to the war in the Pacific he visited a married woman whose husband was already away in the service. Though they "were both lonesome and sick inside," they felt restrained by decency and so squelched their mutual desire to "give and take whatever comfort we had for each other" (19). In writing the book, however, John changed the ending to coincide with a morality higher than the mores of society: "In the story he stayed the night. I wrote it that way because I knew that's what I should have done" (19). So John's rendition of his novel's plot becomes for the audience a prelude of the play's resolution, while providing Katherine with a lesson on being true to one's inner emotional urges to respond with kindness rather than be circumscribed by external codes of behavior.

Anderson lifts the plot for John's novel almost verbatim from a story Ted Jones tells Nan Hilton in *The Eden Rose.* Understandably, any author like Anderson who writes from autobiographical stimuli and moves steadily toward the creation of archetypal characters and situations will use and reuse similar material and motifs, yet once in a while Anderson goes one step further by reusing a favorite passage from an earlier play in a later one. In *Double Solitaire,* for example, Charley Potter's family motto is also *Dum spiro, spero;* but if Sparrow's name provides ample reason for such a motto (as Katherine remarks, "It's nice to have a name so close to Hope" [16]), Potter's assuredly does not. Yet Anderson, perhaps regarding his entire corpus as one long work — as, indeed, there is ample justification for doing — believes such repetitions impart a "resonance" to his work rather than detract from it.[11]

Just as John at an early age compromised his dream of becoming a creative writer, so, too, has the newlywed Philip who, recalling Anderson himself as a young man, wanted a career in music until his father dissuaded him; he is now enrolled in business school but "embarrassed to mention it" since he doubts whether there "can be sincere advertising men" (26). Philip and Janet, both from well-to-do families, are rebelling against the establishment, against parents who "live in a clutter of things with a capital T. Accumulated junk" (26), for they fear being innundated by the success syndrome and ultimately capitulating to it to the detriment of their marriage, as the Websters did in *Love Revisited.* Indeed, from John Bosworth in *Come Marching Home* to Charley Potter in *Double Solitaire*, there exists a strong antimaterialistic strain in Anderson's heroes; with Thoreau, they see the need to "simplify" life by returning to essentials.

More disturbing to John than any compromise of his vocation as a writer, however, is the guilt he experiences over his daughter's accidental death and his wife's subsequent insanity — the closest Anderson has yet come to exploring the motif of man's separation from his wife after Phyllis's death. John, infatuated with another woman, had written her a series of impassioned letters; when the woman finally replied to deny any relationship, John's wife accidentally read the letter. While she sat numbed over John's betrayal, their daughter drowned in a neighbor's yard. Anderson wisely refrains from using this material from soap opera as the main plot of his play, employing it only as an explanation of John's compulsion that he "had driven [Jennifer] insane" (59). Attempting to degrade himself physically so that his outer condition would mirror his inner disgust, he "found solace in sensation": "I wanted to hit bottom. . . . I scavenged off unhappy marriages" (60) — to prove that they could be destroyed just as he had destroyed his own. Even when he now spends a night with a prostitute searching for the "Reassurance, courage, . . . comfort . . . protection against the horrors of the night" (37) that sex can provide, he deliberately guards against any feeling. For John still regards Jennifer as "the condition of [his] life": "the more I tried to destroy the meaning of marriage, the closer I came to its true meaning . . . . Maybe it's guilt that binds me. I think it's love" (61).

But it is, in fact, guilt that predominates over love. And John's excessive guilt is just as destructive as Katherine's unyielding ethical system of the human dimension in any relationship. Like the defrocked minister Shannon in Williams's *Night of the Iguana,* he has forgotten that it is human to sin, but inhuman to become so obsessed with the evil that one can no longer recognize the good in oneself. Anderson, in condemning self-defeating guilt and a sexual morality that puts the letter of the law before the spirit that commands "love one another," writes in *Silent Night, Lonely Night* his most antipuritan play.

That John and Katherine will give themselves to one another before this night is over (even though Anderson, as the minimal forward action of the play necessitated, manages to delay this past the first act curtain) is foreshadowed not only by John's observation that the honeymooners "fill [the inn] with a sort of infectious sensuality" (21), but also by a subdued bit of symbolism shortly after the curtain goes up. When the serving maid brings John's and Katherine's dinners to their adjoining rooms, a sprig of holly stands in a small vase on each tray. After John moves his dinner into Katherine's room and they replace their separate tables with a makeshift one for two, according to the stage directions John "puts the sprigs together, with difficulty" (13), just as he and Katherine will ultimately come "together with difficulty" after much talk of moral scruples.

Part of the delay in their uniting sexually springs from John's insistence, like Tom's in *Tea and Sympathy,* that she not respond out of pity for him or out of any need of hers to feel satisfaction in helping him over a rough spot. But Katherine does not share his hesitation about being loved out of pity; she falls into the category Laura mentioned in *Sympathy* of those who are not unselfish enough to love without getting something in return, and refers to their adultery as "shared sadness" (72). John's calling her by his wife's name during the act of sex, making her in effect Jennifer's surrogate, helps immeasurably to salve her misgivings, for Katherine sentimentally takes this as proof that John does not consider her just another prostitute and as a sign of her potentially regenerative effect upon him: "suddenly I was your wife. . . . For the first time in two years you were sleeping with someone you could care for. . . . it became quite simple and beautiful" (68). With a feeling of "care" added to the purely physical pleasure, they can justify their actions and brace each other for a return to their respective spouses. As Allan Lewis comments: "Sex is again salvation, and the implicit approval of extramarital relations is mitigated by each one's returning to his marriage in the end, better prepared to endure his unhappiness. . . . The Christmas background implied the religious approval of resurrection through adultery."[12]

In *Double Solitaire,* Peter Potter observes that the stories his father writes always end happily: "Do you realize that every single one of your couples gets back together again in the end? Half of them don't belong together. But you bring them back as though you had invented marriage and had to justify it under all circumstances."[13] Peter's observation might be Anderson's self-criticism, for it applies with equal validity to many of his plays, since, with the obvious exception of *Tea and Sympathy, Footsteps of Doves,* and *Double Solitaire* itself, Anderson's couples do get back together again in the end. Yet this seems contrived only in the case of *Days Between* and *Silent Night.* That John completely forgets Katherine's presence in the next room in the joy of hearing that Jennifer is lucid on this Christmas Day is hard enough to swallow; that Katherine decides to forgive Dick's indiscretions and return to him challenges the audience's credibility. Granted, her traditional religious code might tell her that marriage is indissoluble and John's revelation of his loneliness might open her eyes to Dick's need for sex when he is away for extended periods, but Katherine, so far as the audience knows, has given Dick no reason to be lonely within marriage, nor does she have any reason to suppose he will change. Rejecting the notion that his play's ending is sentimental, Anderson relates it to the aftermath of his wife's death:

> The essence of the play was the deeper meaning of marriage . . . and I suppose it was a holdover from Phyllis's last years, when we . . . did have a marriage which was deeper in its hold and meaning than it had been for some time. The point I was trying to make was not to uphold traditional social and moral values . . . but to point out that marriage and its satisfactions involved many more things than the pleasures John had had with Katherine. . . . And I guess this symbolized that I would rather have Phyllis back for a few minutes than have the various possible and present pleasures available.[14]

Anderson attempts to blunt the audience's incredulity at Katherine's returning to Dick by gratuitously bringing onto the stage in the closing moments of the play their son Jerry, a sudden appearance in no way dramaturgically required for the resolution. Along with eliciting viewer response for Katherine as mother, the boy's presence is almost a concretization of why she perhaps stays married. And yet, despite the closing icon of mother and child (appropriate to the Christmas setting of the play), anyone who knows Anderson's work as a whole recognizes how few really *loved* children inhabit his world. Furthermore, the audience must wonder if Katherine's return to her husband can be anything but a further negation of her personality; will she not, somewhat like Laura after the Gentleman Caller has come and gone in Williams's *Glass Menagerie,* be even lonelier than before, having experienced this moment of intense communion? So the play's ending is not as unmitigatedly happy as it appears to be on the surface.

Despite well-drawn and interesting characters coupled with literate dialogue, and despite Anderson's ability to engender compassion for his characters while commenting importantly on love and loneliness and guilt, *Silent Night, Lonely Night* remains unsatisfactory as drama. Tender and touching though it often is (it is not difficult to understand Anderson's own affection for it and to see in the hospitalized Jennifer, who so often might as well be dead since her days of total "living" are so few, the playwright's own traumatic struggle to transmute his personal experience into art), the play's limited action might have been better suited to the novel form. Or perhaps all this should have been exposition for a play not yet written about Katherine's and Dick's marriage after she goes back to him. In fact, a relation similar to John and Katherine's, though not physically consummated, will form a small part of the exposition in Anderson's next drama, *The Days Between,* which focuses on the marriage itself, while relegating something very similar to the John and Jennifer story to the status of a subplot that occurred in the past.

III *Anderson and the American Playwrights Theater*

Anderson wrote *The Days Between* intending to submit it to Elia Kazan, who had directed *Tea and Sympathy,* and Roger Whitehead for possible production in the new theater at Lincoln Center; ironically, the play has never been produced in New York City. Instead, it became the first offering of the then newly organized American Playwrights Theater, playing in college and community theaters across the land during the 1965–1966 season.

The American Playwrights Theater (or APT, as it is usually called) was, in Anderson's term, the "brainchild of Jerome Lawrence and Robert E. Lee," the authors who gave Broadway audiences such successful plays as *Inherit the Wind* and *Auntie Mame.* Aware that economic considerations make Broadway an unlikely "seed ground for new plays, particularly plays of *ideas,*"[15] they determined that "America's practicing playwrights needed an alternate and entirely new platform where their works could touch audiences *not* on the road to Broadway." It was mainly a matter of matching dramatists with audiences and theaters for, given the hit-or-miss syndrome of Broadway, even proven writers might find it difficult, as Anderson consistently has, to get their scripts produced. The intention was never to offer New York rejects to the participating theaters around the country, but rather to make available to them "plays of size, of relevance, of meaning."[16]

The APT contract, "written largely by Elmer Rice" prior to the organization's incorporation in 1964, provided for a selection committee structured to allow the representatives of the producers of member theaters "to decide which plays will be most challenging to the audiences they serve" from among those submitted by working playwrights.[17] Twenty-five member theaters then had to guarantee productions of a play selected by this process before that play would be "activated." During the 1964–1965 season, Anderson reports that "too few subscribers elected to produce the plays submitted by the board."[18] Afraid of the effect that a second season without a production would have on a fledgling organization in which he had great faith and which he was "eager to get . . . off the ground," Anderson reluctantly agreed to allow APT to offer his own new play, *The Days Between,* during the 1965–1966 season, explaining that "For various reasons I felt that my play was inappropriate for college and community audiences."[19] In subsequent seasons, APT has offered such dramas as Ron Cowen's *Summertree,* Lawrence and Lee's enormously popular *The Night Thoreau Spent in Jail,* and *The Last Meeting of the Knights of the White Magnolia,* the first play in Preston Jones' *Texas Trilogy.*

IV The Days Between

Although *The Days Between* eventually became the inaugural production of the American Playwrights Theater, premiering at the Dallas Theater Center in early June, 1965, Anderson conceived and wrote the play originally as a vehicle for his second wife, the actress Teresa Wright, with a view to having it performed on the arena stage of the theater then under construction at Lincoln Center. So this is an instance — perhaps one of the few in modern theatrical history — where the architectural design of the stage, as Anderson has made clear, actually affected and even determined the dramatic strategies, especially the structure, of the play: "I had the feeling, writing for this type of theater with the thrust stage and nothing in the way of realistic sets, that there was a certain obligation to move from climax to climax. You had no excuse for a lot of exposition and a lot of teacups. . . . Maybe it's too much. Sometimes it isn't, sometimes it is, but that's what I'd say is the major problem in the construction of the play.''[20] The multiplication of climaxes within the play is, in itself, neither unusual nor dramaturgically unsound; nearly every play is built not on one continuous increase of tension from begining to end, but rather on several segments of action that elicit from the audience a succession of increases and then relaxations of tensions. Unfortunately, however, the climaxes in *Days Between* — such events as a flower vase flung against a wall, a husband packing his bags and leaving, the ''other man'' offering the opportunity for adultery — smack of the soap opera climaxes that end one segment and keep the audience hungering for the next, to which is added a forced ''happy'' ending.

The adaptability of various types of plays from different periods in theater history to all manner of theatrical presentation belies Anderson's belief that a departure from the box set — such as in *Days Between* with its ''No sets, just levels, lights, and props (5)[21] — prevents dramatizing the trivia of everyday and necessitates that the climaxes come ''bang, bang, bang.'' Whereas some dramatists, such as Thornton Wilder in *Our Town* and *The Skin of Our Teeth,* employ nonrepresentational sets partially in order to break down the illusion of reality and to make the audience aware that they are in a theater watching a play, this is never Anderson's purpose; when he employs a nonrepresentational method of staging, here in *Days Between* or later in *I Never Sang for My Father* or *Double Solitaire,* his intention is to universalize, to strip the theater of its external frills so that the substance dominates. But even when he does use the box set, it is seldom in so simple and straightforward a manner as in *Silent Night, Lonely Night.* As far back as *Come Marching Home,* he had displayed an affinity for the multilevel set, but still within the framework of the representational stage design that attempts to create the illusion of reality; the dual levels in *Marching Home* (part of the room is a few steps up from the rest), in *The Eden Rose* (Nan Hilton's dressing alcove is on a balcony), and in *Love Revisited* (with its balcony over the garden) were perhaps intended to create a greater variety in acting areas, as well as to provide additional visual interest for the audience.[22] Within the confines of the box set even Ibsen, it will be remembered, often achieved multiple locations by requiring a kind of ''inner stage,'' as in *Hedda Gabler* or *The Wild Duck.* The set for Anderson's *Tea and Sympathy,* technically still a realistic box set, similarly permits the audience to see more than one room at a time, achieving complexity by allowing for action on two levels and three locations. Since *Days Between* demands more levels (four) and even more locations (six) it could hardly employ as representational a set as *Tea and Sympathy* does; on the other hand, since it can easily be performed on a proscenium, in the round, or on a thrust stage, it was an attractive offering for APT because of the widely varying physical facilities of its member theaters.

David Ives, the writer-teacher in *Days Between,* has, like John Sparrow in *Silent Night,* reached the "desperate age" of forty (14), but his condition is immensely more harrowing than John's, who has at least come to an accommodation with himself. For David's condition is one of existential angst; like Camus's Caligula, who perceives that "Men die and they are not happy," David feels "this is no place. . . . This is nothing. . . . This . . . is death" (12). Middle age for him is a period of "sour resentment" (14), including sexual impotence and a sense of despair over his inability to actualize the idealistic goals he set in youth, exacerbated by a total lack of communication with his son Roger, reminiscent of the relationship between Dad and Willie in *All Summer Long.* The seminal effect that adapting Wetzel's novel had on Anderson can also be felt in the similarities between Don in that play and David in *Days Between:* like the younger man, David sees his days of glory as retrospective. Also like Don, his hatred of mediocrity leads him to denigrate anything that does not measure up to his high standards.

Returning home a hero from the war, David dreamed of becoming a commercially *and* artistically successful writer who would somehow rise above all the pettiness in the world. Hating mediocrity, believing that there is no such thing as a partial victory or a partial defeat, he counsels his son: "Remember style, Roge . . . . A man's life gets up to here with crud. We weren't sent on this earth just to pay bills, count our change and live in crud" (16). Though his disappointments as a writer have long since plunged him into cynicism and negativism, he was once naively optimistic; his wife Barbara repeats David's favorite philosophic maxim: "'If you have only two loaves of bread left to your name, sell one and with the money buy violets to feed your soul'" (8). The violets that once fed his soul were in the eyes of Barbara, to whom he dedicated his first novel: "'For Barbara and her violet eyes'" (8). When he married her fifteen years before the play opens (this is another of Anderson's dramas in which a celebration generates the action), David had shown her a red silk scarf, the play's major symbolic property, that he had found as a child while living with an aunt in the slums and that is now tied prominently to the lamp in his study. The scarf holds an emblematic power, "His personal banner of defiance against the drabness of the world" and "his promise to [Barbara] that [her] marriage would not be like [her] mother's . . . a promise of ecstasy . . . eternal passion . . . eternal unreality" (47). Thus David suffers from an even more pronounced and longer lasting adolescent romanticization of what married life would be than Roger Hilton did in *Eden Rose;* the improbability of "violet eyes" suggests the impossibility of Barbara's ever being all that David dreamed she would be.

Flower symbolism is once again important. David tells Roger about often buying flowers for Barbara, but no matter how many or how few, they had to be "perfect" because she was "perfect." Now, as their anniversary approaches, David cannot afford to buy flowers, so he sends Roger out to pick some violets. It is, however, too late for violets; in what is a very unsubtle use of symbolism even for Anderson, they have withered, just as David and Barbara's love has. What blossoms Roger can find he arranges in the same vase that contained the very first flowers David ever sent Barbara; yet when David sees the blooms from the florist that Ted Sears, their house guest, has sent, he feels jealous, thinking Ted has deliberately humiliated him. In one of the play's climaxes that holds much the same visual shock as Mitch's and Stanley's tearing of the paper lantern so closely identified with Blanche in *Streetcar Named Desire,* David "slams [his] bowl of flowers into the corner" (21), in effect signaling his responsibility for the destruction of the marriage.

Ted, whose arrival for a writer's conference helps precipitate the crisis in *Days Between,* threatens not only David's estimation of himself as husband, but as father, artist, and writer as well. Anderson here employs the device of parallel plotting more extensively than in any of his other plays except *Double Solitaire.* Although Ted has attained great financial security and popular acclaim as an author of best sellers, David terms his books "successful, sentimental trash" (19). Unlike Ted, David refuses to engage in what he would consider prostituting his writing talent to make money, though Ted (whose novels sound as if they might be of the type and caliber of, for instance, John O'Hara's) harbors no illusions about his own creative ability. George Hawkins, one of David's former writing students who visits him briefly at the opening of the play, serves as a foil to Ted, for he has achieved artistic success but without economic stability. Both George and Ted, in turn, act as foils to David, whose artistic talent as well as financial solvency have dried up. Not realizing the effect his visit will have, George arrives bearing his just published second novel, dedicated to David, "one of the great teachers" (11). The audience senses, however, that George's career will ultimately adhere to the same basic outline as David's, since George, on the verge of marrying, has taken a position "teaching writing" (12). In a lengthy speech (new to the version of the play revised after the Dallas opening) on the demanding vocation of the artist, David — almost certainly speaking for the dramatist himself when one remembers that this was only Anderson's second original play in over a decade — warns George as bluntly as possible about the dangers of compromising his artistic talent by fragmenting his efforts, in thinking that he can pursue a writing career half-heartedly: "Nobody but a writer understands the conditions under which you have to work . . . the ruthless self-discipline . . . the freedom you need. . . . They don't, they can't realize that any day a writer hasn't written something good is a lost day . . . that makes the next day that much more desperate. And when the days become weeks and the weeks, months and years. . . . Nobody can understand the . . . the fear, the panic, that you might never write another line" (13). Unable simultaneously to fulfill his vocation and at the same time to satisfy his other responsibilities by balancing his roles as husband, father, writer, teacher, David almost needs to have Barbara throw him out so that he will have the requisite freedom to write. David's ideal in his vocation, although he must unconsciously sense that his creative powers have burnt out, is hardly more possible than a marriage of "eternal unreality" in a life where nothing smacks of the ordinary.

He also attempts to rationalize away his failures by shifting some of the blame off onto a too materialistic society, just as the Websters in *Love Revisited* and Philip and Janet in *Silent Night* had:

> But there *are* expenses to living, and one part of you knows that . . . the part that is loving and needful. The family part. . . . The artist resents it,

resents the family man and his softness. Yells at him. 'You're no artist. You're a miserable compromiser.' ... Your wife will be jealous of your art, and who can blame her? She will set traps, gentle, loving traps. ... You are Ulysses and she is Circe ... and her song and her loveliness are beguiling. ... The difference is, Ulysses passed the island once. ... The artist never passes it, is never rid of it. ... he wants to give up over and over.... But he can never give up. What the hell would he be if he gave up? Nothing! (13-14)

In *Days Between,* Anderson accomplishes what he had failed to in *Love Revisited,* his earlier — albeit comic — treatment of the same subject, by integrating David's crisis in vocation with his crisis in marriage; for David's lack of fulfillment as an artist, his fear that his first novel may have just been a fluke, exercises a deleterious effect upon his relations with Barbara. Thinking that she married him only because of his promise that he would someday become a greater writer, he believes she has stopped loving him because he has failed. David acknowledges he has not been a good husband, but instead of blaming himself, he hates Barbara for being there to hurt. Impotent as a writer, David is sexually impotent as well, except when he has been drinking; yet at those times, lovemaking is hardly different from rape, a sadistic violation of Barbara, on whom he vents his anger and frustration, as Bill had done to Laura in *Tea and Sympathy.* Barbara understands that the real albatross around David's neck is not herself but a deficiency in him to break out of solipsistic concern with self: "What are you going to write about? ... You don't know anything about life. You hate life ... this life, this ugly but only life.... And you cannot write from hate, only from love, and you ... you are incapable of love or loving. ... You have crucified us all on this dream of yours!" (56). A "dream denied' does not always "dry up like a raisin in the sun"; this dream has become destructive, consuming David as surely as a similar obsession to be Number One consumed Willy Loman.

Even though David Ives remains Anderson's most extensive "portrait of the artist" as middle-aged man, the playwright focuses here primarily not on the writer but on the wife. As Anderson explains: "But suddenly, I think around forty or forty-five, most men, if they grow up, realize that it's too late to start over (not that some haven't, of course). ... And I was fascinated, not to consider it from the man's point of view, but from the viewpoint of the woman who is married to such a man. . . . What does it do to *her* life, to their life, to the children's lives when he suddenly finds himself in a rut, not doing what he wanted to do?''[23] Some years later, after seeing the evening of one act plays, *Solitaire/Double Solitaire,* Vivien Leone wrote with pleasurable surprise at discovering that Anderson was actually a feminist playwright: ''The news about them that went unremarked during their brief run . . . is that they were probably the first contemporary pro-woman plays to have been written, produced and directed by men. . . . Instead of merely complaining, retaliating, or ridiculing, he has actually been paying attention to me and my kind.''[24] In fact, Anderson *had* ''been paying attention'' at least as far back as *Days Between,* consciously written from the woman's point of view. Barbara, as the emotional matrix of the play, is the classic example of the woman who suddenly rebels against being nothing more than an appendage of her husband. She has so submerged her own identity in the socially conventional roles of wife and mother, however freely chosen in the beginning, that she now dreads moving out of the safety and security these roles provide: ''For fifteen years, David has been the condition of my life . . . the reference point for all the love, ambition, hope and guilt'' (46). Without him to provide the sense of being someone — David's wife — she would be nothing.

Barbara had actually left David once before, but a pleading letter brought her running back; like Laura in *Tea and Sympathy,* the woman responded willingly to the man's dependence on her. She had even gone back to work so that David could afford to write, yet he only viewed this as a threat to his masculinity. Barbara's fear of the disorientation of life without David receives bolstering from her mother, Mrs. Walker, who warns her that nothing could be worse than the aftermath of divorce. Her mother's example seems to diminish the options open to Barbara for dealing with David's antipathy toward marriage: ''My father left my mother . . . and overnight her hair turned white'' (40). Instead, she would rather suffer the indignity of ''seem[ing] cheap . . . to hang on to a man because you're afraid . . . to be alone . . . or afraid that no man will ever love you again'' (47). Like Sister Luke in *Nun's Story,* Barbara faces the conflict between commitment to something outside the self on the one hand and freedom to *be* herself on the other; thus her conflict and David's dovetail neatly. If David sees freedom from commitment to others as a necessary precondition to fulfilling himself as a writer, Barbara sees her commitment to him as a threat to developing herself as a woman. Yet, paradoxically, she is "terrified" of the freedom that would come from divorcing him.

Barbara, like Laura in *Sympathy,* is sexually starved: "The nights I've lain in bed crying for an end to desire. But it never comes" (54). She admits, however, to no longer wanting David to satisfy this need and finally confesses that she invited Ted to use their guestroom so that he would "make love to me" (55). In the months before his wife Meg died, Barbara had fallen "in love" with their marriage. This image of their marriage, with Ted so loving and caring, becomes, like David's idealization of the writer's role, her own albatross, an image of perfection she must carry before her as a contrast to the reality of her own married life. Ted needed Barbara's "good opinion" to reassure him what a fine husband he was being during Meg's terminal illness, since "It made [him] feel a little less guilty" for surviving" (34). Yet even while Meg was dying, Ted, as if to strike back at her for deserting him, longed for Barbara, and it was only his compulsion to maintain her esteem that restrained him. Nevertheless, he now chooses to reveal the truth behind the facade of his marriage as a way of saving Barbara and David's, just as Barbara finally shares her secret guilt with David in order to bring about his redemption.

In the manner of the well-made play, the revelation of these two secrets comes fast and furiously in the closing moments of this over-plotted drama. When barbara realizes that she is past the point where a brief encounter can assuage all the hurt (and here she differs from Katherine and John in *Silent Night*), she actually rejects Ted's offer of himself, using him instead as a sounding board off whom she can bounce all her accumulated venom and frustration. She needs to touch a bottom at which all suppressed rage can be verbally exorcised and all masks torn off before she can begin the upward trek: "For years I've been running up and down a long hall keeping doors to ugly rooms shut. . . . Now I want them all to open. . . . I hate my son because he made my husband hate me . . . I hate my mother because she taught me fear" (54). If the hall is her own psyche that has repressed what she could not face, then Ted becomes her analyst-confessor, as David does in the next scene where she reveals what is to her the most "obscene" truth of all: "I killed a child for you. . . . For your dream. . . . A child in my body. . . . I loved you . . . and it was for you, so that you could be free!"

(57). In freeing David, she ironically ensured her own enslavement to guilt.

Ted reacts to Barbara's confession by attempting to renew her faith that something can be salvaged of her life with David through revealing that his and Meg's marriage had also been tempered by fire: "Eight, nine years ago, Meg and I stood at opposite ends of a room and .... yelled at each other our misery, our disillusion ... cried like children for our lost world. ... in time, thank God, we managed to ... crawl to each other. What you saw was .... a kind of re-marriage out of the ashes of our illusions" (60). Ted's confession motivates Barbara to accept David as he crawls back to her, an even less likely thing to happen so quickly than David's destruction of the notes for his novel when he learns of his complicity in her abortion. Both the child, conceived out of his hate, and the book, stillborn because of his obsession with settling for nothing less than "days of glory," must be destroyed before David can acknowledge that even had he been "free" to write he would not have "know[n] what to do with freedom!" (62). David promises to make up for "All the lost years" by "try[ing] to live *now,*" though some question remains whether he will ever be able to "rediscover the wonder of the world like a child," for he still "find[s] it so impossible to live the days between (62–63). As a curtain line, Barbara speaks some favorite words of Anderson's first wife Phyllis, "Nothing is ever really lost" (63).[25] And yet, to render Barbara's readiness to enter into this "re-marriage" with David more convincing, perhaps the playwright would have been wise to retain from the original version Barbara's line that suggested that her act of faith is based on a need to satisfy her desperate physical desire for affection and asserts as well that sex will, as in *Silent Night,* be redemptive. Disputing David's despairing words, "I am dead, Barbara ... dead," she reassures him, "No ... Nothing that stirs such life in me is dead."[26]

Although *The Days Between,* despite Howard Taubman's asseveration after the Dallas production that "It is unthinkable that [it] will never reach Broadway,"[27] has never been seen in New York, it remains, along with *Double Solitaire,* quintessential Anderson, actually more representative than far better dramas like *Tea and Sympathy,* since it contains virtually all of Anderson's major character types (middle-aged writer, disillusioned over his failure to achieve youthful dreams; sensitive wife who attempts to sublimate her own fulfillment, even sexual, by satisfying her need to respond to others), as well as recurrent thematic motifs (lack of communication between parent and child; the redemptive power of sex; the destructive potentiality of romantic dreams; the compromises that inevitably come with time's passage; the opposing pulls of freedom and commitment). It exhibits also both his strengths (structuring by parallel plots and foil characters; considerable psychological penetration) and weaknesses (melodramatic action; forced "happy" endings) as a playwright. Among the latter also must be counted Anderson's tendency to state ideas rather than dramatize them, sometimes in verbose speeches marred by purple prose, for he does not always achieve his ideal of language "drained of emotion, dried down to a bone, but with tears in the audience when they hear it."[28] This play does, nevertheless, hit "close to the heart" of its audiences — as he hoped it would — and, furthermore, provides perhaps the most probing view yet by an American dramatist of what it means to a woman when her identity comes not from within herself as a person but is imposed on her from without.

CHAPTER 6

"Plays for Saturday" — And One for Monday

THOUGH Anderson has often been labeled, and with good reason, a "sensitive playwright," with *You Know I Can't Hear You When the Water's Running* (1967) he hoped to escape the onus associated with that tag, for any such label likely restricts one's audience. In Anderson's case, his plays more often than not do appeal primarily to women and therefore fail to reach the expense account crowd out for an evening's light entertainment. As he told David Ayers, "Suddenly I felt I wanted to write a man's play."[1] In 1966, another of his sensitive plays, *I Never Sang for My Father* — a story for Monday when the audience is in a more serious frame of mind — was making the rounds of producers, as it had been since 1963. As Ayers recounts the story, Anderson hinted during a lecture at Baltimore's Center Stage that his next play might feature its hero coming onto the stage "stark naked with a toothbrush in his hand, saying 'You know I can't hear you when the water's running.'"[2] Though the naked man never materializes in full view of the audience, the result is an evening of four comic plays, aptly described by British critic Stephen Marcus as "a public emasculation of the American male"[3] (whom Anderson always has been interested in cutting down to size).

He originally titled his dramatic quartet "Four Plays for Saturday," and intended that they be produced off-Broadway, for there was then some question whether a group of one acters could be presented successfully on Broadway; *You Know I Can't Hear You When the Water's Running* proved they could, tallying up 760 performances, exceeding the total even of *Tea and Sympathy* and giving Anderson his longest running play to date (Noel Coward had, of course, pioneered the technique of grouping one acters into an evening's entertainment in the 1930s in *Tonight at 8:30*). This is not as ironic as may first appear for, despite the difference in genre that makes the plays more palatable, they are, as Elia Kazan perceived, "'about the same things as [Anderson's] other plays except this time it came out funny and sad.'"[4] Though some critics, especially John Simon who termed the evening "a cento of clean dirty jokes" and found in it "a solidly retrograde mentality at work," regarded *Water* a condescending exercise in tastelessness and vulgarity, Roderick Nordell concluded otherwise: "It is as if, in the midst of the theater's exploration of all that is kinky or bizarre in sexual relations, Mr. Anderson were restoring ordinary conjugal sex as a subject of nonblack comedy. . . . he seems to be putting sex into proportion as a facet of humanity."[5]

You Know I Can't Hear You When the Water's Running was not the first time Anderson had essayed the comic sketch, reminiscent of the vaudeville routines he had seen at Boston's Old Howard while a Harvard student. His first work seen by Broadway audiences was, in fact, a seven page satirical skit about the theater called "The Lunts Are the Lunts Are the Lunts," in Dwight Deer Wiman's short-lived 1950 revue *Dance Me a Song*. In that sketch, Alfred Lunt and Lynn Fontanne despair of ever finding a suitable new vehicle; Lynn assures Alfred they should take heart: "Worse come to worse, you can always play the father in Arthur Miller's new play," because "There's always a father in Arthur Miller's new play." Among the available scripts, Lynn finds a phone book and, recalling a complimentary comment that they could draw an audience merely by reading a list of names and numbers, lights on the idea of doing precisely that. In a prophetic note, she says they will engage Elia Kazan to direct (which Anderson would do for *Tea and Sympathy*), since "'in the weak spots he'll give it such pace that no one will know or care what's being said'"[6] The rest of the skit has them acting out the phonebook in the grand manner, with great verve and passion.

I The Shock of Recognition

Walter Kerr, one of *You Know I Can't Hear You When the Water's Running's* staunchest admirers, begins his essay on "Nudity" on the contemporary stage by "wonder[ing] if Robert Anderson ever wants to take it all back. . . . He was the very first person to suggest, however whimsically, that a theatrical producer *might* want to send an actor out on the stage in the nude."[7] Anderson espouses his "whimsical" notion in *The Shock of Recognition,* where an intelligent and commercially successful comic playwright named Jack Barnstable discusses with his producer the difficulties of casting his latest endeavor, which features a man coming naked from the bathroom to remind his wife: " 'Honey, you know I can't hear you when the water's running.' " (9)[8] Within two seasons of Anderson's playlet, the suggestion had become a widely publicized reality in *Hair* and *Oh! Calcutta!,* and so Anderson's sketch, in which the actor auditioning for the role strips down to his shorts before Jack calls a halt, quickly became, as Kerr appraises it, "quaint indeed, fuddyduddyish even."[9] But if Kerr regarded the whole thing as an amusing but harmless lark, John Lahr harshly berated the playwright for "operat[ing] on the ... dynamic of Puritan titillation, toying with the flesh but never actually believing in it."[10] Yet Anderson's latest play, *Double Solitaire,* and his novel *After* help belie Lahr's charges of "prissiness" and "puritanism," unless one argues that Anderson becomes clinically explicit in those works to cash in on the profits of the new sexual candor.

It would be fairly easy, however, to regard the conclusion of *Shock of Recognition,* with an audience of disappointed voyeurs seeing only the "right hand" of the "naked" actor's body, as a cop-out, except that one realizes that Anderson does not regard nudity itself as important, but employs it here as a metaphor of the artist's vocation as a barer — and bearer — of truth. As Anderson explains in an interview, " 'The closer I come to a certain nakedness, the better I write. ... I think this other kind of nakedness that Spender talks about, the nakedness of emotion, personality, psyche, etc., is far more important than physical nakedness.' "[11] At some risk of attributing too much weight to this one acter, it is Anderson's most detailed exploration in dramatic form of the art he practices.

If the play is performed today, the remaining humor derives not from the passé situation but from the energy and inventiveness with which Anderson's best comic creation to date, the out-of-work actor unromantically named Richard Pawling, tries to convince Barnstable and the producer Herb Miller that he is perfect for the part — and not just this part, but any part. An actor for all seasons, infinitely adaptable, unlimited in his range of characters,

Pawling can be either tall or short, well-built or weakling, tan or pale, with long hair or short, and that either dark or blond. And he has no difficulty in identifying with what Barnstable asks him to do in his play, for he has done it in real life: "that's a situation I know like the back of my hand" (20). But even if the novelty of the idea has been diluted by recent happenings in the theater, *The Shock of Recognition,* picking up a thread from *Tea and Sympathy,* remains Anderson's sharpest attack on the myth of the virile male.

Barnstable describes himself "as a serious playwright ... not someone just out for kicks and shocks" (9) — an assessment that applies equally well to Anderson — and so feels that audiences will understand "It's not as though I were trying to do something sexy" (4). He intends to destroy once and for all the stereotyped image of the aggressive male held up by society for emulation, a point reiterated with unnecessary frequency in such a brief play: the central character in Barnstable's comedy "is not a sexy, muscular man ... bare to the waist and full of erotic implications as to what he's got in his bulging blue jeans. I want to show man as he is .... I don't want an Adonis on stage. That's what the movies and the other boys are getting at" (5-6). Miller seconds this, but in a sarcastic way: "Barnstable wants .... in a sense, everyman .... he wants to present his man not as a stud, not as a romanticized phallic symbol, but as the miserable, laughable thing it is" (22–23). Barnstable's intent is to show naked man "with no implications except of mortality and ridiculousness" (6) — the first of which, anyway, corresponds to David Storey's emphasis on man's vulnerability and finitude in *The Changing Room,* which contains (even more so than Peter Shaffer's *Equus*) arguably the most artistically justifiable use of nudity yet seen in the theater. Here Barnstable's point (and Anderson's, too) is that for a man to become obsessively preoccupied with his sexual organ as "a work of stunning magnificence .... a formidable weapon .... to attack with" (7–8) is perhaps the greatest romanticization of all and the one most injurious to understanding that masculinity involves sensitivity as well as strength.

Yet Barnstable himself is held up for ridicule on two counts, with the consequent danger of deflecting the audience from seeing the truth of his notion of manhood and of art. First, though he wants a nude actor in his play, he is embarrassed to discuss the role with Pawling and constantly refers to the male genitals with the

euphemistic "it." Second and more damning, Barnstable — a dramatic descendant of Charles Webster in *Love Revisited* — holds an inflated notion of the importance of his nude actor in the history of drama. He feels that singlehandedly he is forcing the theater to mature and twice compares his contribution to Ibsen's: "I think it can be one of the great moments in the history of the theater ... Like Nora slamming the door in *A Doll's House*" (21).

Anderson agrees, as Barnstable says twice, that the essence of the dramatic event is "the pleasurable shock of recognition," a moment of "honesty and truthfulness" that prompts an audience to respond, "'My God, that's just like us'" (21, 4). This comes close to being Anderson's artistic credo as well as Barnstable's; both are "saying to the audience ... 'Do you believe in life as it is lived? ... Don't you want to see it?' I think they want to see the ironies, the paradoxes ... the absurdities ... Hell, Life is a tragedy played by comedians. ... Let them see it onstage" (15). This serious human comedy is what Anderson gives his audiences.

II The Footsteps of Doves

Of the four short plays, *Footsteps of Doves* is the most perfectly crafted and consistently amusing, yet, one suspects, least substantial and likely to endure — if any of these sketches can be expected to endure, since they stand, in reality, very close to television skits in scope. Anderson, conscious of the visual impact of the dramatic form and of the way that inanimate objects can become part of the cast of characters, gives the audience almost the entirety of *Footsteps* in their first glimpse of the stage set: the scene is a basement showroom of a bedding store, and "At one side there is the usual double bed: fifty-four inches. At another side, there are two single beds" (31). The double bed, connoting togetherness through physical intimacy, stands in conflict against the twin beds, associated with the separation resulting from the physical distance between people. The dialogue contrasts the virtues and drawbacks of both, and the lighting as the curtain falls helps declare the double bed triumphant: "The lights fade, but last of all on the fifty-four inch bed" (51).

Harriet and George, who for twenty-five years have slept in a double, are shopping at her insistence for twin beds. Anderson uses Harriet and George's waning sexual relationship to make two comments central to his philosophy of marriage: First — and by no means a new motif, going back at least as far as *Eden Rose* — though sex is not the only means of contact between a married couple, no marriage can survive intact and be mutually fulfilling for very long without it. As Anderson says, "You will note through all the plays that I really do believe that there are many ways of communicating . . . but I don't rank talking above sexual affection and emotion. For centuries women have established this false hierarchy. . . . Talk first . . . sex later."[12] Second — and this motif achieves final formulation in *Double Solitaire,* of which *Footsteps* is essentially a preview in a comic tone — while normal practice regards the woman as more romantic in her outlook than the man, Anderson suggests that, at least for the adolescent and again for the middle-aged male, it is the other way around. Furthermore, in *Footsteps* Anderson does not condemn George, who wants the comfort of sex more just at the time his wife's desires decrease, for attempting to satisfy his physical needs elsewhere.

Harriet, whose symbol is the twin beds, feels that her wanting to be left alone is a permanent condition, since she believes that her age and the physical changes her body is undergoing necessitate a dulling of her affectionate side as well. But the visual image of them squeezed together on a twin bed in the showroom should prove that twin beds will not suffice even for the infrequent times when she might desire George. As if this were not enough, his verbal equation of two people together in a single bed with being in a coffin — "Put sides and a lid on it and bury us" (33) — leaves no doubt that this will kill their marriage. George understands that this seemingly innocent shopping spree signals a critical turning point, commenting: "Neitzsche said the big crises in our lives do not come with the sound of thunder and lightning, but softly like the footsteps of doves. . . . I can hear the doves!" (37, 42). To make the conflict not totally one-sided and Harriet not wholly unsympathetic, there is the implication, however, that their double bed has allowed George — more interested in having sex than in making love — to take her too much for granted; as she remarks: "Old everready . . . . I may want the space so that you'll have to make the effort . . . . Not just suddenly decide you might as well since you hardly have to move to get it" (40).

George stands at that dangerous and potentially promiscuous age where the only thing preventing his looking elsewhere is the comfort provided by the double bed. All day long, he must "bump up against hard facts, hard edges, cold bodies" (34) that he seeks refuge from at night. He views the move to twin beds as analogically related to the depersonalization of contemporary life, and he discovers a kindred soul in the young divorcée Jill, who also senses the diminishing quality of life.

Jill serves as a perfect foil for Harriet as well as a perfect match for George, since she is "an indiscriminate snuggler" (47) and, what is more, a firm mattress and morning person like him. Her former marriage both contrasts with what George and Harriet's used to be and previews what it will become, for her ex-husband, tied to his mama's apron strings, saw the single bed as a pleasant continuation of bachelorhood and less of a commitment. Unable to afford a double bed just now, Jill becomes the "charity" to which George will donate his and Harriet's old one. In contrast to the earlier scenic image of Harriet and George crowded uncomfortably together on the twin bed, the picture of Jill and George on the double bed foreshadows their affair. The salesman comments at one point, "Last week a couple broke off their engagement right here" (36); now a marriage is broken off. Harriet has won the proverbial battle, but lost the war. As George says to the double bed when he and Harriet leave, "Be seeing you" (51).

III I'll Be Home for Christmas

The reviewers generally found the third one act play the most developed and substantial; some even expressed disappointment that Anderson had not chosen to expand *I'll Be Home for Christmas* into a three act drama, taking full advantage of its possibilities for pathos. Yet for Anderson to have done so would have made abundantly noticeable the play's basic structural flaw — its lack of resolution; it now ends with the reading of a letter that, in a full length drama, the playwright might have used to begin the action. Here Anderson attempts something complex and perhaps too subtle for a play meant primarily for entertainment, since the central conflict is not what it appears to be up until the last few mintues — a dispute over how to deal effectively with sex education in the family, a subject explored earlier in *Eden Rose, All Summer Long,* and *Tea and Sympathy,* where the fathers fail to provide their sons with the necessary answers and proper attitudes. Rather, the central conflict is occurring in the mind of the protagonist, with the only hint of this inner conflict coming in the surreptitious transfer of a letter from a shirt to a trouser pocket. The effectiveness of the play depends on the audience's noticing that switch and their resultant curiosity about what he is hiding.

In *Christmas,* Edith Berringer returns home one afternoon to discover her husband Chuck unexpectedly back from work. The "living room and kitchen of [their] modern apartment [is] represented by no more than a couple of flats" (55) — a fitting set for a play in which the Berringers, up to a point, might be figures in a cartoon entitled Mr. and Mrs. Middle America (this is, one might add, Anderson's only "blue collar" play). But the "brawny" beer drinker can be every bit as sensitive underneath as the intellectual writer-teacher type so familiar to Anderson audiences; like John Sparrow in *Silent Night,* Chuck has taken to pondering "the meaning of it all." As a concerned Edith tells her friend on the phone, Chuck is "at war with the inevitable" (56), just another way of saying that he is up against the passing of time, the waning of opportunity, the loneliness as children leave the nest, the knowledge of mortality, the disillusionment that comes from self-assessment — all things he is sorely equipped to understand.

Yet Edith wastes no time in berating Chuck for failing to talk with their youngest child Timmy about the facts of life, though her surface insensitivity may be a defense against dealing with more unsettling matters "that frighten her to death" (55). Not wanting Timmy to feel guilty about masturbating, Edith wants Chuck to explain that it is "a normal, healthy part of his life" (59). If necessary, Chuck should even confess that *he* masturbated as an adolescent so that Timmy will not think he is somehow failing his father whom, like several typical sons in Arthur Miller dramas, he idolizes. To this problem, Edith adds a further annoyance: she wants Chuck's approval to have their daughter Clarice, no longer a virgin, fitted with a birth control device. Anderson would side with Edith's insistence that sex must be discussed forthrightly; but if she does not, unlike Ruth in *All Summer Long,* want to portray sex as dirty, neither does she, unlike Nan Hilton in *Eden Rose,* have any conception of doing this with the love that will emphasize it as something beautiful.

Edith's attitude, instead, reflects the recent proliferation of sex technique manuals, for she divorces sex from human feeling, reducing it to something mechanical, as it became for the Bridgers in *A Small Part of a Long Story.* It becomes purely appetitive, "a natural hunger," Edith says, "and just as with our other appetites, we satisfy them as best we can . . . under the circumstances" (60). Edith praises her own father for having been open with her about sex, but his explicitness was on the same level as Herb Lee's in *Tea and Sympathy.* Rather than the enlightened and liberal twentieth century mother she considers herself to be, Edith might accurately be called a hedonistic utilitarian: one's instincts rule man; no one can rise above his nature; the more erogenous zones that can be satisfied, the better. She even expects Chuck to be unfaithful to her — it would be somehow unnatural and even less than manly for him not to be.

But Chuck is faithful, for if every other facet of his life seems to be crumbling around him, he demands that meaninglessness not invade the center of his life: "Here in the most personal and private core of me, I insist that there be meaning" (74–75). He knows that sex is more than a question of "how-to"; it involves "tenderness and affection" as well, and he refuses to be party "to destroy[ing] the beauty of sex" (66). He realizes also, as Don did in *All Summer Long,* that the best way to educate one's children is through example: "When's the last time, if ever, they caught us necking on the couch? That's the demonstration we should give them" (68). In a statement that surely encapsulates Anderson's own sexual ethics, Chuck says: "sex is beautiful . . . one of the great blessings of mankind . . . in all its forms . . . as long as it involves no coercion, or injury, or pain . . . to anyone" (61–62). All questions about the rightness or wrongness of sexual acts in Anderson's works must be referred back to this point.

The pathos generated by the play's closing moments arises from the audience's awareness of Chuck's insight and sensitivity and yet his inability to communicate this love to his children — Anderson's way of once again decrying the stifling of emotion by the American male for whom masculinity means restraint. When Clarice enters, she brings a copy of the letter Chuck hid at the opening; it is from the oldest child Donny, away at college. As she reads it aloud, the audience's attention is pivoted on Chuck's expression. Donny has written expressing his complete rejection of the father's system of values: "I think you've been preparing me for the only kind of life you know. . . . but I could never take that kind of life. . . . You all fought a war. . . . But after that, what happened? . . . I don't want it to happen to me. . . . Sometimes I don't know how you have the courage to get up in the morning'' (77).

After hearing the letter, the audience feels deeply for Chuck because it understands the full ramifications of the play's title. *I'll Be Home for Christmas* expresses the dream that sustained those men as they fought; but in the period since their return, the values they defended have crumbled. Things that seemed within reach then are impossible now, and the realization of the little distance he has come pains Chuck. He can only close his eyes as "his voice breaks": "if only in my —" (78). In the last minutes, Anderson confronts the audience with his archetypal middle-aged man all over again.

IV I'm Herbert

Of the quartet of short plays that comprises *Water, I'm Herbert,* while little more than a revue sketch (only twelve pages and even fewer minutes to perform), comes as a surprise to audiences familiar with Anderson's persistent themes and techniques. Nowhere in his previous writings does one find any interest in the theme of time's effect upon memory — though attitudes toward time's effect upon idealism and sexual desires have been prevalent — and the only work even remotely like it in technique is the farcical "The Lunts Are the Lunts." *I'm Herbert,* with its banal and hardly coherent ramblings of the old couple Herbert and Muriel, was immediately compared with the works of Ionesco. Yet if there exist noticeable technical similarities (Anderson disclaims any conscious imitation)[13], in its metaphysics it belongs not at all to the Theater of the Absurd, still most succinctly defined by Ionesco in his essay on Kafka as "'that which is devoid of purpose. . . . Cut off from his religious, metaphysical, and transcendental roots, man is lost.'"[14] For in Anderson's playlet, it is memory, albeit dulled and confused by the passage of time, that provides man with a sense of continuity and a saving mooring in the universe.

In structuring *I'm Herbert,* Anderson displayed his fondness for music by deliberately using as his model the Bach fugue, with the ordinarily contradictory and usually repetitious memories of the crochety and slightly senile Herbert and Muriel played off contrapuntally, one against the other. Each has been married at least two

— and possibly three — times before, unions of varying sexual gratification: Herbert to Grace, Mary, and maybe Helen; Muriel to Harry, George, and perhaps Bernie. And so the possibilities for mistaken identities in the realm of the mind are practically endless, providing opportunities for a whole string of verbal gags, limited only by the actor and actress's ability to keep all the names straight (one mistake and they would never find their way back to the script) and the audience's patience at seeing all the permutations worked out. Addressing each other by the name of one of their previous spouses becomes symptomatic of the pair's inability to distinguish between present and past — and also between the recent past and the remote past. As Muriel admonishes Herbert, whom she calls Harry: "Lovey, you're running a lot of things that happened at different times together now" (90). The persistence of memory, ironically even failing memory, multiplies possibilities at the same instant that ongoing time diminishes the number of new ones yet to come, permitting Herbert and Muriel to be seven couples instead of just one and to share together more than they could ever possibly have experienced in any one relationship.

Only tangentially a play about old age, and the harmless rather than sobering side of senility at that, *I'm Herbert* is even less a statement about lack of communication, though that motif does tie the four one acters together and makes sense of their overall title, *You Know I Can't Hear You When the Water's Running.* True, both Herbert and Muriel accuse each other of failing to hear distinctly, and little verbal spats ensue when each refuses to budge from attesting to the certainty of their uncertainties about the past. The final effect, nevertheless, remains not one of pathos over memory's decline, but instead one of happiness over the fullness of their life together as she becomes all his wives and mistresses and he all her husbands and lovers, defying the usual quantitative limitations that time imposes.

If earlier they argued over whether they "were in Venice together" (83) or ever carried on "under the willow tree that June" (88), or ever "pranced around in the nude" (87) with one another, now the precise circumstances of these events no longer matter. An elegiac glow hovers over the play's close:

HERBERT (After a long moment) Mmmmm . . . Venice.
MURIEL (Dreamy) Yes . . . . Wasn't that lovely . . . Oh,

you were so gallant . . . if slightly shocking . . .
(She laughs, remembering)
HERBERT The beach . . .
MURIEL The willow tree . . .
HERBERT (Smiling) You running around naked . . . Oh,
lovely . . . lovely . . .
MURIEL Yes . . . lovely . . .
(They go on rocking and smiling, holding hands as the
lights dim) (91–92)

The tonal quality of the close of *I'm Herbert,* as well as the central theme, is reminiscent of another short Pirandellian sketch written at about the same time, Harold Pinter's "Night," which also casts the audience in the role of amateur sleuth, searching for objective truth, until they realize, as here, that the subjective truth of memory may be infinitely richer and more rewarding. Pinter's playlet ends with the man, aware of his wife's needs, which differ from his own, acceding to the truth of her memories, even when they involve other men; in doing so, he participates creatively in her memory world, thus continually renewing their marriage. As Anderson remarks about the old couple in his play, they "drift off together," he having "accepted the role of all the other husbands or men that the wife ever had" and she having "accepted the role of all the other wives or women that [he'd] ever had."[15] Paradoxically, Herbert and Muriel's marriage, passed beyond physical sexuality, is the most satisfying and happiest in all of Anderson's mature works.

V I Never Sang for My Father *On Stage*

In *The Days Between,* Barbara Ives, speaking with a young author, mentions that her novelist-husband David believes every writer starting out must pen his "'God damn the father book'" (8). If Anderson, nearly fifty-one when *I Never Sang for My Father* opened in 1968 (giving him, for the second time in his career, two plays running simultaneously on Broadway), is hardly a fledgling dramatist, this patently autobiographical work might still be considered his "damn the father" play; for only here does the conflict between father and son — specifically the artist-son — that has been hovering in the wings since *All Summer Long* and *Tea and Sympathy* finally come center stage. Gilbert Cates, who produced the drama on stage and later directed the film version, in asserting that the "battle for primacy of soul, for the right to live life one's own way, is the theme of *I Never Sang for My Father,*"[16] could just as easily have been characterizing a drama that, in both technique and theme and to a lesser though still noticeable degree in language, *I Never Sang for My Father* greatly resembles, Tennessee Williams' *Glass Menagerie.* Though Anderson denies that he had Williams' drama in mind as a model, the resemblance was hardly calculated to work in his favor. After a disappointingly brief run of 124 performances in New York, *I Never Sang for My Father* opened in London, where Frank Marcus spoke for a host of reviewers and theatergoers when he wrote, "It is sensitive, intelligent, patently honest — and very stale and familiar," while Irving Wardle stated more bluntly, "We have met these people before."[17]

The fact that *I Never Sang for My Father* was originally conceived and written as a filmscript entitled *The Tiger* affected the play's structure, for although Anderson had adapted drama and fiction to film, this marked the first time he had adapted a screenplay for the stage. He saw a need for some device to achieve narrative continuity by bridging the different locations in the filmscript and finally settled on having the middle-aged son, Gene Garrison, function as narrator. Five times in Act One and twice in Act Two, Gene "comes down[stage] and addresses the audience" directly (3),[18] sometime to indicate — as the Stage Manager in *Our Town* or Alfieri in *A View From the Bridge* or Tom Wingfield in *Menagerie* do — the time and location of the scene. (Except for essential props, "there are no sets. Lighting is the chief means for setting the stage" [3].) Sometimes, too, the narrator, provides necessary exposition in this drama that is long on exposition of a past that cannot be changed but might be better understood and short on forward-moving action. Sometimes, particularly at the beginning and end, Gene also suggests his own reaction and/or guides the audience's response to the material. Anderson felt that *I Never Sang for My Father* "worked very well on stage with its scenes dissolving in and out of each other with the son-narrator bridging the dissolves"; nevertheless, he believed that he "could never completely disguise the fact that the story had first been conceived as a film."[19] It appears doubtful, however, that anyone not knowing this beforehand would guess that the play had not been intended for the stage all along; if far from original, the mechanics still impress one with their simplicity and fluidity.

I Never Sang for My Father, like Tennessee Williams' *The Glass Menagerie,* is a "memory" play or examination of conscience, all of the action occurring within Gene's mind. Both are likewise guilt plays; but whereas Williams' autobiographical protagonist finds release from his guilt over having forsaken family responsibilities to answer the equally demanding imperative of self-fulfillment when his sister blows out her candles at the end, Anderson's autobiographical character Gene seems unlikely ever to feel a similar forgiveness for having failed, in his own estimation, to love his father adequately. Near the opening of the play, Gene tells the audience: "Death ends a life but it does not end a relationship, which struggles on in the survivor's mind towards some final resolution" (3). This suggests that the play is yet another attempt at achieving that wished for "resolution." When Gene utters practically the same words at the end, the audience knows that the exercise has not proved therapeutic for Gene. The guilt remains.

Yet what was there, really, that he could have hoped to sing about in his father anyway? Dozing quietly in front of the television set, Tom Garrison looks to be "a touching picture of old age"; as a personification of some abstraction called "father," he possesses a "sad dignity" (79). Once paternalistic protector of the lair, but now no longer needed in that capacity, he has become the Old Tiger, who makes Gene alternately want to rage in anger and cry in pity. For with his wife and children Tom exudes the aura of a brigadier general: authoritarian, opinionated, patronizing, egocentric, unsympathetic of others' failings, and, what is more, cranky with age. His gruff exterior may, however, be a defense against an inner sense of emptiness and guilt that surfaces unconsciously when, for no apparent reason, he quotes some favorite lines: "'All's lost, all's spent, when we our desires get without content . . . 'tis better to be that which we destroy, than by destruction dwell with doubtful joy'" (39–40).

Tom's father had deserted his wife and children and, when she died, Tom, seeing himself as defending his mother, literally shoved his father off the funeral coach. Though ordinarily embarrassed at openly expressing emotion, Tom almost maudlinly nurtures his grief over his mother's death. His fondest treasure from the past is her picture, and when he cries decades later over the death of his wife Margaret, he mourns even more his mother's passing. The sorrow for the two losses is very nearly indistinguishable when, in the coffin showroom, Tom sees a child's coffin that recalls his mother, a little slip of a thing. (In this scene, Anderson brilliantly demonstrates the economy of means at the dramatist's disposal in creating illusion by having "Shafts of light in the darkness indicate the coffins" [71].) Contrasting with Tom's sentimentalizing of his mother's death is the bitterness and spite over his derelict father's, whose dying request was for some oranges; Tom sent them, but only a few since he knew the man would soon be dead. It is this lack of reconciliation between father and son that, because of its finality, burdens Tom with unresolved guilt. Gene perceives that Tom hated his father, and he tries desperately not to repeat the pattern of hatred in their relationship. Both Gene's guilt over somehow failing his father and Tom's over having hated his are magnified because each is fixated with the memory of a mother whom they loved too much. Jo Mielziner, who designed the stage setting for *Father,* with his usual insight evidently saw that the *liebestod* of the entire action was a dual Oedipus complex, for Anderson disparagingly found the set "pretentious, as if I'd written Oedipus or something."[20] In his unproduced and unpublished play, *Love Among Friends* (1956), which appears to be partly an early version of *I Never Sang for My Father,* Anderson made the Oedipus motif explicit in an exchange between another father, Mr. Hamilton, and his successful playwright-son Alan: the first remarks: "'It might be interesting to look at the Oedipus theme from the point of view of the husband and father. What does such a relationship between a mother and a son do to the husband-father?'", to which the latter retorts, "'Or how does the attitude of the husband-father towards the wife mother create the climate for the Oedipus situation? . . . . I love my mother as I love you. . . . But I don't thank you for letting me be a mother's boy.'"[21] So *I Never Sang for My Father* is as archetypal and mythical as it is personal.

Tom's values are part and parcel of the American dream of success, values that his daughter Alice, whom Tom ostracized for marrying a Jew, labels "phony" (97). And if *I Never Sang for My Father* recalls *The Glass Menagerie* in its memory structure and its theme of responsibility, it is equally like Arthur Miller's *Death of a Salesman* in its rhetoric and in its revelation of the failure of the American dream, as well as in making the father-son confrontation the core of the play. Linda Loman's admonition to her sons that they must respect their father Willy in her "attention must be paid" speech finds an almost exact carbon copy in Margaret Garrison's rhetoric in *Father,* in lines such as "Everything he's done, he's done for his family" (31), and even in some of Gene's dialogue, like "Still he's my father, and a man. And what's happening to him appalls me as a man" (85).

Although *I Never Sang for My Father* is less a social problem play than *Death of a Salesman,* many of the same aspects of the American system that Miller scrutinizes and condemns for victimizing the little man are also examined, albeit more implicitly, by Anderson. Tom, like Willy, attempts to make his life conform to and reinvigorate a myth — in his case, the myth of the Old West that he is mesmerized by over and over again on TV; throughout his life he has invariably cast himself in the role of the good guy on the white horse striking down the villain (his father on the funeral coach) who besmirches the heroine's honor. Anderson here debunks the myth of the West, just as earlier he debunked the destructive side of sports through the excesses of Herb Lee and Bill Reynolds in *Tea and Sympathy* or of military might through the paranoia of Collins in *The Sand Pebbles.* Added to this, Tom sees himself as living proof of the American belief in self-reliance. His life, a mix of bits and pieces of America's historical and fictional past, has been a microcosm of the country's progress itself: a rags-to-riches romance that has ended in disillusionment, an exile from the garden because of the sins of materialism and emotional shallowness. A latter-day Horatio Alger hero, whose regimen for self-advancement reminds one of Jay Gatsby's in Fitzgerald's novel, Tom discovered his philosophy of perpetual optimism in Teddy Roosevelt's advice: "'Obstructions, yes. But go through them or over them, but never around them'" (69). The watchword for iron-willed Tom has always been that no obstacle is ever too great so long as one never says "quit": "Any young man in this country who has a sound mind and a sound body, who will set himself an objective, can achieve anything he wants, within reason" (69–70). And since Tom has achieved every *material* thing he ever wanted, he is not disillusioned in the same way as other Anderson characters who have sought less tangible goals.

But Tom did, in a sense, "say quit" when it came to Margaret. Ironically, he fails to see that he is guilty of doing the very same thing he so detested in his father: if he never deserted his wife physically, he did desert her emotionally. Because Tom failed to satisfy her needs, Margaret, like the mother in *All Summer Long,* has turned increasingly toward Gene, who shares her interests in music and the theater, as a substitute source for the affection she should have received from her husband. And while Gene, like Don in *All Summer Long* (many motifs from that play are reiterated here), understands that "A son is not supposed to make his mother's life" (78), Margaret, for her part, sincerely "tried not to be one of those possessive mothers" (36), though her closeness to Gene is part of the reason for the gulf between father and son, a situation made more evident in *Love Among Friends.* Alice perceives the ambiguity in Tom's feeling for Gene, who is an extension of his father and thus potentially a means of securing immortality, but who is also equally a threat to the father: "Don't you understand he's got to hate you? He may not think it in his head or feel it in his heart, but you are his enemy! From the moment you were born a boy, you were a threat to this man and his enemy" (97). Tom, jealous of his son's youth and sensitivity and the satisfaction he has found in writing and teaching, casts Gene in an adversary role; perhaps subconsciously, he also desires him to fail as a son — just as he wants to deny him the chance to succeed as a husband by standing in the way of Gene's remarrying — for then Gene can share in Tom's guilt over his own failure as son and husband. As Henry Hewes wrote, the drama's "most interesting area" is "the way we all manipulate each other by guilt."[22]

Now eighty, Tom suggests to Gene that they will have "some time together at last. Get to know each other" (92). What might conceivably make that belated attempt a viable possibility is their shared grief over lost mothers and wives, though Tom seems to forget that Gene ever had a life as a husband. But the possibility diminishes because of the two men's ambivalent attitude toward death. Tom paradoxically feels jealous of those who will live on after him, yet pities himself for having survived his wife and thus having to live alone in fear of his encroaching death. And if this is a late date for Tom to get to know his son, it is an equally late date for the middle-aged Gene to go in search of his father, whose advanced age underscores Gene's own "intimations of mortality." After their mother's death, Alice (whom Anderson has said is the voice of Gene's other, less-concerned side[23]) believes their only responsibility is to see that the father is "taken care of"; her "responsibility" now "is to .... husband and .... children,"

(83), to the present and future, not to the past, which is understandable in light of Tom's denial of her. Yet if Alice is perhaps too unfeeling, she accuses Gene of ignoring his responsibility to himself by being overly sensitive of his "need to love" the father (85); she counsels Gene to "accept the inevitable sadness of this world without an acute sense of personal guilt" over not "ruin[ing] our lives for an unreasonable old man" (96) who has, in effect, attempted to emasculate his son.

Gene, however, wonders if there are limits to his responsibility and finds it onerous to relinquish his moral sense — or is this, as Alice claims, just an indulgence on his part to buoy up "the image ... of the eternally bereaved husband ... forgive me ... the dutiful son ... They're very appealing and seductive ... But they're not living" (99). In the final confrontation (which Anderson added during rehearsals of the play and which he claims never to have had with his own father[24]), Gene makes "the most loving gesture" he "has made to his father in his life" (106) by asking Tom to come and live with him and his new wife and stepchildren, only to be rejected by a petulant old man who demands things on his terms or not at all. Gene's rational and hard side finally wins out over his emotional and softer instincts as, taking his sister's lead, he accuses Tom of "want[ing] to possess him ... entirely and completely!" (110). In so doing, Gene (and Anderson as well) may partially be transferring what he knows but cannot bring himself to admit are faults of the mother, whom he never blamed for possessiveness, onto the father.

If Gene has failed to love his father, it is not through lack of trying, and yet he cannot forgive himself. So the audience may justifiably wonder if the play is ultimately much more than a masochistic exercise in self-pitying laceration, given the portrait of Tom that the dramatist sketches. The cause of Gene's troubled conscience is, as Alice wisely perceives, what might be called the curse of the ideal, or, as Joseph McBride terms it in another context, "a sentimental regret for being less than perfect."[25] And although Gene, torn between what Robert Heilman would call "conflicting imperatives and self-assertive impulses,"[26] appears to be potentially tragic, Anderson — who normally eschews the tragic mode in favor of the melodramatic one — instead of allowing Gene to reach "self-knowledge, acceptance of guilt, and ultimately forgiveness of self" (again, Heilman's terms) sentimentalizes him into a man who victimizes himself by indulging in self-deprecation. But Gene's obsession with his inability to "sing" for his father is only half the story — and only half the reason for his irresolution at the play's conclusion. For in assessing his conduct as son, he has neatly submerged and repressed his conduct in his relationship with his deceased wife Carol and his possible failure in that relationship. It is this possibility that comes to the fore in the screen version of *Father* and becomes the focus in Anderson's novel *After.*

VI I Never Sang for My Father *on the Screen*

Less than three years after its brief Broadway run, *I Never Sang for My Father* was finally released (1970), with greater success, in the medium for which it had initially been written, with Anderson's filmscript restored to its original state, but including now the climactic confrontation between father and son added during rehearsals of the play. Anderson remarked, "I think the material feels very happy to be back in its original form — a screenplay,"[27] and his instincts about *Father* working better on film than it ever had (or could) on stage are basically sound. However, except for the more objective, and thus less melodramatic, manner in which the film handles its material, there is not as much difference as the comments of Melvyn Douglas, who portrayed Tom Garrison in the movie, lead one to expect: "'They tried to get me to do *I Never Sang for My Father* when it was first a play, but it struck me as dangerously close to soap opera. . . . But when the film came along, every single reservation I had about the play seemed to be solved in the film script.' "[28] A close examination of the two versions reveals that the dialogue is virtually indistinguishable, so that everything said above about the play's content — though not the form — applies to the film adaptation.

The major changes are basically two. First, Gene's narration, used in the drama to achieve fluid transitions between scenes, appears only at the very beginning and again at the end of the film, and then only as a voice over. This creates greater immediacy by making the audience forget almost completely that Gene is recollecting past events. Edward Anhalt, himself an author of such screen adaptations as *Member of the Wedding* and *Becket,* comments, in a remark that explains the difference in effect between *I Never Sang for My Father* on stage and screen, that a heightened sense of reality differentiates the cinematic experience from the theatrical: "When you go into the theater there is a covenant between you and the proscenium arch, which is agreed upon tacitly. . . . But at all times, you are aware that you're in the theater and you're going through that mutual process. On the contrary, when you're going to a film, a film is never really successful unless you forget where you are, completely, and are totally involved in a very realistic sense with what's going on."[29] And since visuals now replace the narrative sections, *I Never Sang for My Father* no longer strikes one as so derivative of *The Glass Menagerie.* Gene's report, however, of escaping from the house after his father's rejection — "That night I left my father's house forever. I took the first right and the second left, and this time, went as far as California" (158)[30] — still seems verbally and tonally to echo Tom Wingfield's "I didn't go to the moon, I went much further. . . . I left St. Louis. I descended the steps of this fire escape for a last time,"[31] as surely as the shot of the "Light in Tom's window go[ing] out" (158) visually echoes the similar shot, symbolic of death, at the beginning of Orson Welles's *Citizen Kane.*

Second, certain sequences either difficult to stage — Gene's affair with Norma or his visits to various homes for the aged — or simply requiring additions to the cast — Gene's fiancée Peggy — that were removed in the play have been restored in the film. Peggy's presence gives the viewers an outsider's perspective on Tom that makes explicit one of the keys to his success, the way this man whom his children see as so overbearing can impress casual acquaintances; to her, "he's charming" (133). Gene regards Peggy literally as "a breath of spring," thrusting him from the world of the aged and dying into one of youth and vitality, so that he remarks to her, "Make me a promise . . . let's die young" (123), when she arrives just after the sequence in which he inspects first a private nursing home and then a state hospital. The documentary quality of this segment jars badly with the style of the rest, making it obvious that this is primarily a didactic statement about the way Americans treat their elderly parents — a shift in tone that need not necessarily have occurred had the audience later simply seen Tom in the hospital.[32] As his plea to Peggy makes clear, Gene's visits to the hospitals have heightened his own awareness of mortality; Robert Lifton and Eric Olson eloquently capture in their book *Living and Dying* the way that seeing parents die affects Anderson's middle-aged characters: "On the life watershed of middle age, one becomes aware that life is not unbounded at the far end. The boundary of one's death is suddenly no more distant that the boundary marked on the other end by one's birth. ... one has always 'known' that one would die, but now this knowing becomes a compelling individual realtiy."[33]

More substantive than Peggy's presence is the brief scene of Gene in bed with Norma, which in the play had been reduced (because it could not be easily staged) to the two line exchange between Gene and his mother when she euphemistically inquired if he was "communicating" (34). Here, Gene can verbalize to Norma his contradictory impulses: anger at his father's impossible demands ("it's just that I get so fed up being treated like a child .... by that senile old man" [62]), yet, simultaneously, his guilt at the prospect of walking out on him ("He's a forgotten man in an ungrateful city. ... It depresses the hell out of me" [63]). Having begun his affair with Norma while his wife Carol was dying, Gene feels guilty, not so much for having been unfaithful, but for "using" Norma — whom, he thinks, must consequently hate him — as a release for sexual tension and a comfort in his loneliness. Norma, evidently knocked around by the world, takes a pragmatic, even cynical, view of the relationship, understanding that sex need not always be an expression of love, and counseling the overly idealistic Gene not to demand sentimentally of himself that he give so much to his sex partners: "Only you want to set it [the world] all right. Make it like in the story books, love eternal beyond death. ... and sex always an expression of abiding love" (64).

Since the substantive alterations from play to movie are so minimal, what accounts for the qualitative difference bewteen the two and consequently for the audience's deeper emotional involvement with the film version has to do in this instance with the nature of the cinematic medium, particularly with its use of closeups and shifting points of view. On film, these characters, while more objectively seen, are also more individualized, whereas on stage they seem too often the abstract, allegorical father, mother, son, as if Anderson were attempting to give us archetypes rather than to invest concrete human beings with a universal resonance. As Edward Murray comments: "On the stage characters incline to be types and even symbols; on the screen characters tend to be more individualized and realistic."[34] The uniformly fine acting and

Gilbert Cates's strategy in directing helped also to bring about a difference in perspective from the play. As Cates describes his method, "The style of the film is direct and largely nonsubjective. Nothing must stand in the way of the audience's growing awareness of the interaction between the two men."[35] And nothing does in what ranks with *The Nun's Story* as one of the best films made from an Anderson screenplay.

CHAPTER 7

The Theme is Loneliness

ALTHOUGH Winifred Dusenbury does not discuss Robert Anderson in her excellent book, *The Theme of Loneliness in Modern American Drama,* Anderson's plays do focus, like those of his contemporaries Tennessee Williams and William Inge, on the lonely man "psychologically isolated from satisfactory human relationships."[1] And not just loneliness, but particularly middle-aged loneliness has been Anderson's special métier from *Tea and Sympathy* on, culminating in his two most recent works, an evening of one act plays entitled *Solitaire/Double Solitaire* (1971) and his novel *After* (1973). About the former, the dramatist has said: "Though the plays differ enormously in style, they deal with the same theme: loneliness. 'Solitaire' is about the loneliness of being alone, and 'Double Solitaire' is about the loneliness of marriage."[2] And one of the characters in *After,* which examines the loneliness that pervaded a marriage now ended by death from cancer, echoes the author's statement of his theme by remarking: "I think I'd rather put up with that [the loneliness of not being married] than the loneliness I sense in most of the marriages I've seen" (184).[3]

I Solitaire

Anderson's *Solitaire* serves as a paradigmatic exploration of the pervasive isolation he sees as a distinguishing mark of the contemporary human condition. Set in an antiseptic futuristic technocracy, à la Huxley's *Brave New World* and Orwell's *1984,* the play examines the enforced breakdown of the institutions of marriage and the family that once formed the basis of society. People are denied not only their self-identity — males have a ten digit identifying number plus their combined sperm count-intelligence quotient — but any attachment to other persons or places as well; like the sisters in *The Nun's Story,* they are prevented from inhabiting the same "cell-like room" (3)[4] for any extended period of time that might foster a feeling of belonging or being rooted. Their only escape, which the "system" that exercises complete control does everything to make socially desirable, is to opt for early self-disposal, by which the already identityless person can choose, in the only exercise of individual free will that remains possible, to become a physical nonentity as well.

Fifty year old Samuel Thomas Bradley, number 1783.965.281 IQSQC240, can, unfortunately, recall the way things were before the system ensconced itself; he still retains a picture of his wife Florence, who pressed the self-disposal button after the state took their five year old son for failing to pass his qualifying examination, and he can "communicate" with her disembodied voice on the ironically named "Marriage-Minus-One" tapes. Marriage no longer exists, nor do sexual relations now that children are conceived through artificial insemination. Such depersonalized sex, along with the state psychologists' prescription of autoeroticism as a cure-all for one's anxieties, plunges Sam deeper into loneliness and makes him feel little better than an animal.

The only panacea — and a pleasantly novel touch in an otherwise predictable play — comes from Sam's availing himself of Call-Families, the system-sanctioned houses of illusion where Sam, old enough to be desperately nostalgic for the affection and sense of identity once provided by the family (a nostalgia, by the way, that women no longer experience) can pretend for a few hours that he is still somebody's son and husband and father. These brothels of the future, presided over by a madam, are reminiscent of Genet's *The Balcony*[5] — except that here only the chief of police is permitted to engage in sex; other patrons are simply supplied with replacement families trained to engage in stereotypical situations or to recreate religious or patriotic or family festivals (so important to Anderson) now largely forgotten in a society where even birth and death have been robbed of their dignity through selective breeding and disposal of the aged and other deviates from the norm.

Denied the joys of knowing his own son, Sam wants to experience an illusory "Father's Day"; but since it is a particularly busy night, he must settle for a pregnant girl dressed in a storybook outfit of fourteen to act the role of his daughter. She, however, thinking it is Christmas, "sings very simply, but without feeling or understanding" (18) a chorus of "Oh, Little Town of Bethlehem," signifying that religious belief no longer functions as a viable support for man either. The madam agrees to make an exception by allowing Sam some tenderness and physical display of affection, even though her employees have never experienced this under any but simulated conditions; real affection is also to be feared since it could awaken an emotional side alien to these Skinnerlike programmed people. Despite the banality of Sam's conversation with the woman playing his wife and the squabbling between the son and daughter, he treasures these evocations of home and says a prayer, almost identical to Mother's in *All Summer Long,* thanking God "for the beauty of the Family, the loving closeness" (24). The audience, meanwhile, is clearly intended to recognize that this parody of domesticity actually mirrors their own stultifying existence.

Sam's anxiety increases with the certainty that the boy playing his son really *is* his son. But the police captain feels equally certain that the boy is *his.* This intense desire to find the son becomes more striking when set against several earlier fathers in Anderson's works who ignore or fail their sons. The boy, however, cannot cope with the prospect that he might be the son of either of these men, for such a relationship would demand an emotional commitment foreign to him. Yet Sam searches not only for the son, but embarks on a mythic search for the father as well, specifically requesting that a father be added to the family circle. So an old man who donned a Santa costume for the Christmas Day illusion in the next room is brought in (perhaps underscoring that in America the father's love is often measured by material things). When he cannot remain, Sam himself begs to be kept on in the madam's house to play the father. Anything, even a retreat into illusion, is preferable to the pervasive loneliness.

When refused, he returns to his sterile cell, more than ever aware that he "just [does not] like it here anymore," that "A man can't live this way!" (32). In his despair, he lunges at the self-disposal button, in what is hardly a conscious choice. Nevertheless, some vestiges of his humanity still accrue to this "nonperson," for he finds it impossible to take the proffered suicide pill. Rather, he dies deprived of air, symbolic of the way the system has suffocated his humanity.

As a dystopian vision — though Anderson disavows that the creation of an anti-Utopia was his main purpose[6] — *Solitaire* is not imaginative enough to be very chilling for audiences familiar with works like Rex Warner's *Wild Goose Chase,* Ray Bradbury's *Farenheit 451,* or Anthony Burgess's *A Clockwork Orange.* Furthermore, as Catherine Hughes' review suggests, "'Solitaire' [is] empty at least of any development of its idea beyond banality."[7] And the futuristic setting of the work makes it a somewhat unlikely curtainraiser for the longer, and far superior, *Double Solitaire,* with which it displays a jarring and perhaps disorienting contrast in style.

II Double Solitaire

Generally, the critics responded more favorably to the second one act play on Anderson's twin bill: Henry Hewes judged that "'Double Solitaire' contains Robert Anderson's best writing to date," while George Birrell in the *Edinburgh Evening Standard* concluded that "rarely can the subject [marriage] have been treated with such startling insight and compassion .... This is a tremendous play, deeply moving yet deceptive in its simplicity."[8] Although not a popular success on Broadway, it has since been widely acclaimed on public television and may yet deservedly come to be seen as Anderson's finest dramatic achievement since *Tea and Sympathy* nearly two decades earlier. Certainly it stands as his most imaginative and original in conception and a fitting culmination to his dramatic output thus far.

In response to the persistent question about what ails the contemporary commercial theater, Anderson usually diagnoses the problem by replying that "the matter with the theater is that the manner has become the matter,"[9] by which he means that striking exterior forms have become an end in themselves. To prevent this in *Double Solitaire,* Anderson strips the outward trappings down to a minimum, in line with Walter Kerr's dictum that "logically art begins in a taking away. ... that will enable [the artist] to suggest more with less. The deletions .... open the door to a second imagination, the viewer's .... the more he must do for himself, the more deeply engaged he becomes in the work."[10] So this play serves as a culmination of Anderson's movement away from illusionistic or representational stage settings that he had begun in *Days Between* and *I Never Sang for My Father.* Yet even when writing dramas that are nonrepresentational in their staging, Anderson always demands from his audiences an acceptance of the characters and events as real; in other words, though the room might not always look real, the people who inhabit it most assuredly are. With the hindsight that *Double Solitaire* affords, it becomes clear that Anderson deliberately delocalizes his scenery in order to render the "matter" of his plays more universal.

This tendency to move in the direction of archetype is nowhere more apparent among Anderson's works than here, where as a source for his structure the dramatist returns to the form of the early morality plays. As might be expected given the allegorical form in which characters embody or personify certain abstract attitudes, Anderson's *Double Solitaire* has sometimes been judged as little more than a case study for a psychology textbook or a group therapy session; more than one reviewer found this play for the very married "a symposium on marriage [rather] than a dramatic treatment of its pros and cons."[11] And indeed, much of the time it does, as Martin Gottfried suggests, tell rather than show,[12] substituting explicitness for the subtlety that many consider synonymous with art.

Married for twenty-three years, Charley and Barbara have been asked by his parents, Mr. and Mrs. Potter, celebrating their golden wedding anniversary, to renew their marriage vows along with the older couple as part of the elaborate festivities. Lacking any belief in religious ceremony, Charley cannot accede casually to his father's wishes; besides, it would be hypocritical to do so, since time has widened the distance between Charley and Barbara rather than welded them together. To visually reinforce this estrangement, the two sit through most of the play at separate tables, unaware of each other's presence, as each of the remaining characters successively "comes from the shadows," speaks his lines, and then "moves back into the shadows" (37, 40). These other characters represent the possible options or choices open to Charley and Barbara and thus have some kinship with the tempters in a morality play. The first three-quarters of the play might profitably be viewed as a psychomachia in the minds of Charley and Barbara.

The stoppers-by at Barbara's table, who speak lengthy, unanswered monologues to a mute Barbara, are both female: her mother-in-law, and her divorced friend Sylvia. Even if Mrs. Potter, a proper "patrician" of "seventy-one," "has missed a great deal of life and knows it" (37), she conceals this awareness and disillusionment under a mien of philosophic calm. She actually finds pleasurable the gradual lessening of intensity in her life, showing what Nan Hilton in *The Eden Rose* would have become had she married Oliver Sexton. Oblivious to her husband's physical needs, Mrs. Potter believes that the sexual side of life ends at menopause, that the period after fifty is a time of decay. In a poem she loves to recite, she expresses what would appear to be a proper acceptance of the cyclical nature of time: "'Tis well when old age is out, / And time to begin anew'" (40). Death is not to be feared, for without death there can be no rebirth. And yet, there is something more than just readiness for death in Mrs. Potter's attitude; from Anderson's point of view, she started the withdrawal process years before her time and revels too willingly in the drift toward death. Subterfuges such as her garden, her church, her poetry readings, keep her from recognizing the emptiness of a life drained of physical and emotional contact. The games of double solitaire she and her husband play symbolize perfectly the loneliness, the inadequacy that Mrs. Potter is sadly oblivious to — within their marriage: "each of us lays out his own deck, but you put the aces in the center as they come up, and each builds on them ... The play of the cards is lively. ... It gives us something to do together" (40). Though she has considered divorce, she has always accentuated the reasons for staying together, as she counsels Barbara to do: "In every marriage more than a week old, there are grounds for divorce. The trick is to find, and continue to find, grounds for marriage" (39).

If Mrs. Potter's "grounds for marriage" are the security and calm it affords, Mr. Potter's are the ethical conventions about abiding by vows ("I put great store by form and routine and ritual" [44]), even if this involves a degree of sham. As Mrs. Potter suspects, her husband is, like most of Anderson's men, more romantic and idealistic than the women they are married to — or at least they maintain their youthful romanticism longer than their wives do: "It's a romantic idea, this renewing the vows. But then men *are* the romantics, so full of nostalgia for the past they thought was so happy" (39). Despite opportunities to do otherwise, Mr. Potter, a seventy-five year old "gentleman of the old school" (40), who possesses a strong puritan streak and is endowed with a pragmatic respect for traditional institutions like marriage, has remained faithful to his wife. Thus his only advice to Charley is to compromise and make do with what he has, keeping a stiff upper lip: "accept the situation and find your own way to make it work. . . . A dog whines. But a man doesn't whine" (45).

After having listened to the viewpoints on marriage held by a couple older than themselves, both Barbara and Charley next hear from friends of their own age who tempt them to violate the moral and social norms espoused by the parents. Barbara's recently divorced friend Sylvia suggests that dissolution of an unsatisfying marriage is the best course. If she felt lonely within marriage — and probably caused her husband anxiety by being "a very boring wife" — now with a succession of male friends for each day of the week she at least no longer "has time to be lonely" (48). In a remark that surely strikes home for Barbara, Sylvia says that in her experience men only mention marriage "at just about the time they're getting tired of making an effort. They're ready to take me for better or worse and for granted." So she "much prefer[s] to be a visitor in a person's life" (49) rather than embark on any more lasting arrangement. In this way, abiding by a philosophy diametrically opposed to the placid acceptance of Mrs. Potter or the biting-at-the-bit endurance of Mr. Potter, she can satisfy her certainty that "life was meant to be lived, not just endured" (50) — words that echo those of Jack Barnstable in *Love Revisited.*

Sylvia has opted for divorce; Charley's friend, George, however, wants the personal and sexual freedom she has while maintaining his marriage, at least in name, and thus tempts Charley with his code that adulterous affairs are really preferable to divorce. The latter finds himself especially vulnerable to this advice since he has been writing passionate letters to Maria, herself a recent divorcée and young poetess whose books he edits. But whereas George can have meaningless sexual flings without any emotional attachment, Charley, less cynical about marriage and an idealist like his father, feels a compulsion to search in every relationship for "A woman about whom I could feel and continue to feel with such intensity that my whole life would take on meaning" (53).

The family's third or younger generation, represented by Charley and Barbara's twenty-two year old son Peter, believes, in contrast to Charley's father, that form and ritual has in itself no meaning whatsoever. Peter's watchwords are "freedom" and "anarchy" and "joy," and Anderson provides no easy synthesis between these and the grandfather's standards. For Peter, only the private commitment between individuals, unwitnessed by anyone but themselves, matters; not legally bound by or to anything outside themselves, Peter and his "wife" Melinda will then not have to be loosed by anyone. They believe, naively, that this will insure an easy and painless "split" if the time ever comes to separate.

Though Charley and Peter disagree on many points and follow divergent lifestyles, at least they do communicate with one another, and when they are critical of the other, it is in a positive and loving way. Significantly, it is only after Anderson exorcises the ghost of the father and airs all the hatred and resentment between Gene and Tom in *I Never Sang for My Father* that he can dramatize, for the first time, a close and mutually respectful relationship between father and son. Charley and Peter are most alike precisely in their romanticization of sex in marriage and in their belief in marriage as a means of establishing one's identity. Both Charley and Peter say, in effect, that they were "nothing" before they met Barbara and Melinda. Yet as Anderson's works consistently show, there is an inherent fallacy in making someone else the "condition" of one's life to the point where that other person must shoulder the blame for one's own failures; marriage cannot create a feeling of self-worth where none existed in the first place.

The sentimental and tenuous basis of Peter and Melinda's relationship becomes apparent to both Charley and the audience as Peter shows the three minute movie he has made. Entitled "I'm Home!", "the film is a lyrical evocation of a young man's coming home in the evening to the girl he loves" (67) — his getting off the bus, stopping to buy the evening paper and a bunch of flowers, running down the street and bounding up the steps to an apartment where he finds his girl in the bathtub: "We draw back quickly and stop action on the scene, the girl in the tub, the young man kissing and fondling her ... and the flowers floating on the surface" (68). Walter Kerr, for one, found the film's inclusion within the play ambiguous: "We are left without an attitude toward it.... It is simply there, an object, well observed .... In the end it is without significance, and that is what is troubling. We *want* to take an attitude toward it, to have a feeling about it .... I would like to have known what to think of that film. Knowing, I might have cared more."[13] And yet, neither this short film nor the slides of Charley and Barbara's marriage which both Mr. Potter and Charley flash on the screen — and which Douglas Watt insisted "add neither information nor visual interest"[14] — are merely Anderson paying lip service to the use of multimedia effects in the theater. In fact, they are the key to the dramatist's point of view in the play and as such can only be omitted from a production at great risk. For they demonstrate that Peter and Charley are cut from the same fabric as Mr. Potter; all three adhere to an incurably "idealized, romanticized, and sexualized image of marital bliss,"[15] much more so than do the women they marry, which is one of Anderson's original insights into the male-female relationship and a point of view not often expressed in literature, which tends to see females as the real romantics.

Charley's main difficulty in his relationship with Barbara is his adolescent fixation with sex; from her point of view, he has never outgrown the pubescent obsession of boasting about his sexual prowess. As Barbara says, "You sound like a bunch of kids with a toy. Look at my Yo-Yo" (73). Charley has never matured to the point where he can communicate with Barbara or express affection for her through anything *but* sex. But now she is going through a period when the physical is less important to her — "All brides die" (82), though Anderson would say "some brides hasten their own death and the death of their marriages"[16] — and so she sees Charley as exploiting her by turning her into an object that he uses and abuses, thus in essence reducing intercourse to a masturbatory act. Seldom has anyone since Strindberg written so candidly for the theater about the male-female conflict in marriage. But whereas Strindberg focused on the man's emasculation at the hands of the woman, Anderson here explores the woman's victimization by the man in a continuation of the thread he began in *Days Between.* Barbara Potter says, "I hate marriage. I hate what it's done to me. I'm not me. I'm a nice person, loving, warm, gracious, understanding . . . when I'm not married" (80). Is this Barbara, who would rather have marriage without sex than settle for sex without love, a more mature Barbara Ives ten years after she decided to *stay* married?

Anderson does not force a happy ending on *Double Solitaire* as he had on *Days Between.* This play — with Barbara revealing to Charley that separation could not make her feel "as lonely as [she has] been these last Goddamned years" (82) and saying "I'm not sure I care if we do . . . stay together" (83) — ends more ambiguously, suggesting that Anderson's vision of marriage has itself undergone a process of maturation through the very act of examining it so incessantly in his writing. Perhaps the loneliness within marriage can become so overpowering that it outweighs the fear of being alone outside marriage — a position that Anderson seemed reluctant to admit after *Tea and Sympathy,* though he was groping toward it in *The Footsteps of Doves.* With its open-ended dénouement, *Double Solitaire* strikes one as being Anderson's most unsentimental and uncompromising play to date.

It also contains the fullest treatment of his favorite recurrent character, the middle-aged writer (this time by avocation rather than vocation) — another in a long line of alter egos for the playwright himself. As such, Anderson handles him sympathetically, even to the point of claiming in his extradramatic comments that it was not his intention "for Barbara to be victimized by Charley,"[17] Not only is Charley a middle-aged author, but he is "man in the middle,"[18] poised between age and youth, editing and writing, commitment and anarchy, responsibility and freedom, wife and potential mistress, marriage and divorce, loathing and love, self and selflessness, with little chance of coming to any synthesis. As George puts it, "We're transitional figures, Charley. And it's rough to be a transitional figure" (57), for it means in essence being set adrift from all one's spiritual moorings. Charley, the archetypal Anderson male, is a middle-aged everyman — a schizoid, fragmented product of the contemporary age who "desperately long[s] to be just one 'me'" (59), a divided self searching for integration. As a symbol for his condition, he adopts the play's prevailing metaphor: Robert Frost's line, "Two roads diverged in a yellow wood" (54). One cannot travel two roads at once, and Charley understands that to choose one at the expense of the other necessarily means to be haunted forever by a sense of lost possibilities. Every existential choice one makes limits the range of all one's future choices, for each time one chooses A over B, one's options at the next moment of choice are automatically halved; if one chooses A, the possibilities that would have opened up if one had chosen B are lost forever, and vice versa. Anderson's close friend Elia Kazan comments similarly about another middle-aged man: "Well, by the time you're fifty-four, there's no eraser left on your pencil's end. You're condemned to those choices you made before you knew they were choices. All you can do is pay for the trip you've taken."[19] This notion of diminishing possibilities — what might be called after Frost's poem "the road-not-taken" syndrome — is a recurrent motif in modern American drama; it forms the basis of what has been too loosely called O'Neill's deterministic philosophy and appears prominently in the plays of Albee, particularly *A Delicate Balance* and *Seascape.*

Because of Charley's and Barbara's opposite attitudes about sexuality — he seeing it as a means of confounding the existential void, she as a source of increased loneliness — the poetic image, "Two roads diverged in a yellow wood," ultimately becomes, like the game of double solitaire itself, symbolic of their marriage: Charley traveling one road, Barbara another, and Anderson here accepting that distance with all its implications rather than insisting on any facile solution. *Double Solitaire* seems a culmination and deepening of all his dramatic output since *Eden Rose* and might have been his finest achievement in dramatic form, surpassing even *Tea and Sympathy,* were it not for the nagging feeling that sometimes one is listening to a tract rather than seeing it embodied in dramatic action. But it is still visually impressive and superbly moving on stage. Little wonder that when Anderson sits down to write today for the theater, he "suddenly stop[s] and say[s], 'But I've written all this'"[20] in *Double Solitaire* — a work he terms "the synthesis of everything I know about the theater"[21] — and so has turned increasingly to fiction.

III After

Instead of titling his first published fiction *After,* Anderson might have appropriately called it "I Never Sang for My Wife" since, like his play of three years earlier, it focuses on the survivor's (in this instance, the husband's) attempt to discover "some resolution" to the guilt and self-recrimination that remain after a marriage ended by death. Like Gene Garrison in the drama, the novel's first person narrator, himself a novelist named Christopher Larsen, doubts at the close of his extended self-examination that any easy resolution can be found: "But I know that for many years, perhaps the rest of my life, no matter where I might be, I would be standing here waving good-bye, and wondering" (342). After several works in which the death of a spouse remains submerged in the past or peripheral to the central action — *Tea and Sympathy, The Days*

Between, I Never Sang for My Father, Solitaire — the wife's death from a lingering illness and its effect upon the survivor here become paramount.

Although Anderson considers *I Never Sang for My Father* his most autobiographical play, *After,* evidently written from the same therapeutic motive that prompted Gene Garrison so incessantly to pursue an end to guilt, seems finally to be the work in which its author's autobiographical impulse is strongest. Just as it takes Larsen, his creator's alter ego, "years" before he is "able even to try to write about" his wife's death (9), so, too, it took Anderson fifteen years before he could undisguisedly transmute into fiction his ambiguous response to Phyllis's death, though he had attempted to do so earlier: an original, unproduced filmscript dating from 1964 and concerned with "the legend of a writer's marriage and the death of his wife"[22] appears to have been an early draft of *After.*

The title Anderson finally chose for his novel points to what he regards as its emphasis — life, not death, the survivor rather than the victim.[23] The first third of the book that focuses on Fran Larsen's death could (and this is one of the novel's structural weaknesses) be divorced from the remainder, which details Chris's affair with Fran's young protegé Marianne Chappelle, and stand on its own as a beautifully controlled and crafted, if unresolved, novella about what has been called "the last taboo." Read apart from the rest of the novel, it might be seen as the fictional counterpart of such popular works as Elizabeth Kubler-Ross's *On Death and Dying* or Lynn Caine's *Widow*. In a sparse and understated style that contrasts sharply with the effusive and often inflated prose of the later two-thirds, Anderson charts the contradictory feelings of love and hate, self-sacrifice and self-pity, acceptance and anger that beset Chris as he ministers to Fran through five years of slow suffering from cancer and the mingled rage and self-reproach that accompany her death: rage first at having to face her pain and then at her having left him alone, then guilt over living on after her; self-reproach for all the times he wronged Fran, who can no longer offer forgiveness. In words that echo Ted Sears' in *The Days Between,* whose life story is a miniature of Chris Larsen's, Chris says: "The survivor is the sinner and cannot forgive himself, and the only person who could forgive is gone" (10). When Fran takes her own life rather than suffer further debilitation, leaving a letter begging Chris not to revive her if he arrives in time (which he does) but to remember their long-standing promise to "have the decency to let the other one go ... [to] even help" (31), he resents being burdened with this responsibility. Nevertheless, his complicity in her euthanasia receives less attention than the reader expects. Despite Chris's avowal, "I knew I would go over and over that moment the rest of my life, wondering why I had let her die" (33), he does no such thing, leaving the reader to wonder why this plagues him so little during the remainder of the book when questions of sexual ethics trouble him so often. The answer may lie in Chris's feeling that by unselfishly granting her wish and allowing her to die, he is making recompense for all the times he failed Fran during their life together.

Fran, as actress, friend, wife who gave unstintingly of herself and "never refused a call for help" (57), had become a legend in her own time, and Chris's vocation after her death — despite her former acting teacher's warning that he "'mustn't make a life out of tending a legend'" (114) — becomes that of keeper and embellisher of her memory in order to assuage his guilt. Again like Ted Sears in *Days Between,* Chris needs other people's good opinion of him as a husband; yet, in the very process of trying to keep the legend inviolate, he begins to question the veracity of that picture and to see the hurt they inflicted on one another in the name of love. When Anderson reflected upon his experience as a widower in an essay, "No Final Curtain on the Ghosts of Grief," he wrote: "There are two lines of Spender's that express [the] attitude of the surviving husband very accurately: 'At first you did not love enough / And afterwards you loved too much.' The danger is one of idealization. Because it is difficult to live with the image or memory of the inevitable cruelties and meanness in any marriage, one tends to create a legend of perfection, still, oddly enough, remembering one's own cruelty — and you begin to believe your own lies about the relationship."[24] If Herbert and Muriel in *I'm Herbert* are far enough along into senility to remember only the good things — or, as seems more likely, to have harmlessly falsified the reality in their confused memories of the past — Chris is too lucid and compulsively honest to resort for long to subterfuge.

In *Days Between* and *Double Solitaire* Anderson explored the fate of women whose whole identity derives from their role as wife; in *After* he details an opposite and equally relevant situation: what happens to a man who lives always in the shadow of his wife. Chris admits he "was dependent on [Fran] for the quality of [his] life" and had "no life independent of [her]" (127). He always wrote only to "please her," to make her "proud," to fulfill her "expectations" (64). During her illness, caring for her became his "whole existence" (37), a martyrdom he willingly embraced. Even after her death, she exerts her hold over him, since his life's meaning becomes synonymous with spreading her legend. Whether consciously or not, Fran, who never wanted to display any dependency on him despite his need to "know she needed [him]" (311), actually emasculated him. And he inadvertently aided her in this by his neurotic compulsion, like Gene in *I Never Sang for My Father,* to be the ideal husband to the point that he demanded that their relationship be drained of the least inkling of selfishness on his part. His compulsion kept him even from asserting himself sexually for fear of simply using her. Consequently, he did not satisfy her sexually, which meant that she could then patronize him by saying that this did not matter anyway, which only made him feel even more inadequate. Fran's cancer becomes, then, symbolic of the lack of "real intimacy" (15) that has eaten away at their marriage.

After her death, Chris "wanted Fran back so that [they] could play it all over again and have it different" (168), and he gets the chance to do this, in a sense, through his relationship with Marianne, the first recipient of an acting scholarship established in Fran's name. Marianne views the affair as a means of participating vicariously in their "life together," as "her way of sharing something she felt was beautiful and sad and romantic" (251), while Chris, on the other hand, eventually comes to regard her as a surrogate for Fran, in much the same way that John had Katherine in *Silent Night, Lonely Night.* Having reduced the *cogito* to "I feel sensation, therefore I am," Chris enters upon the relationship as a reaffirmation of his life after having lived so long with death. Love and Death, Eros and Thanatos are the parameters of his existence: "This part of me [sex] was going to lead me back to life, was going to insist on living" (197). Understandably then, if Anderson is to convey Chris's narcissistic exuberance in youth returning to his body through sexual arousal and gratification, there is need for a number of clinical passages; indeed, one factor that determined that this story would be told in novelistic rather than dramatic form was his awareness that the material demanded too explicit a treatment for the stage.[25] Unfortunately, as even one of the less high-pitched examples will illustrate, these sexual descriptions, instead of reaching poetic heights à la D. H. Lawrence, are often puerile and embarrassing, a nearly fatal flaw in a book whose subject is sex: "With a cry that was half a groan I entered her. . . . She would allow no control, no waiting, no technique. With a kind of purity she insisted, and gratefully I accepted and selfishly drove on to my own release" (136). What Chris's affair with Marianne forces him to acknowledge is his inability to unite sex with love and to love unselfishly; his obsession to prove himself through sex (he has not escaped from the myth that sexual prowess and masculinity are synonymous); and finally his tendency to enter into emasculating relationships.

Chris searches always for a woman who embodies the Strindbergian ideal of wife-mother-whore; for example, with Marianne he experiences "Odd quick changes of feeling, sometimes to want to be with her as a man, flaunt the pleasure of my reawakened virility, sometimes to want to be held and comforted" (184). Though uncertain that he can ever be giving enough to be truly a husband (Fran echoes Barbara about Charley in *Double Solitaire* when she says about Chris that he makes a better lover than husband), neither in marriage nor outside of it does he find the sought after fusion of roles in his sex partners: Fran is primarily mother, partly wife; Marianne is partly mother, primarily whore (not in any moralistic sense of the word). Chris is acutely aware of his tendency toward selfishness in his sexual encounters when he tries to subjugate his partner as a compensation for his battered ego. Marianne, on the other hand, might at first seem like Laura in *Tea and Sympathy* or Katherine in *Silent Night* — a ministering angel helping out a needful man; yet she is less altruistic than either, desiring to become as nearly as possible another Fran, filling her place both on stage and in Chris's life. She also displays a predatory side in her professional behavior, as seen in her treatment of the older actress Ruth, who attempts to seduce Chris as an antidote for self-pity; however, Anderson's handling of the jealousy between ambitious ingenue and aging actress resembles the Margo Channing–Eve Harrington conflict in *All About Eve* and seems stereotyped by comparison.

What, on the surface, precipitates the break between Chris and Marianne, along with further estrangement of Chris from his son

David, comes directly from a soap opera plot: during the divorce proceedings of Chris's friend Jean, some passionate letters that he wrote her while Fran was dying, "'running down [their] marriage'" (310), are made public. But the real reasons for the gulf between father and son and lover and mistress are deeper. In the former case, there has always been a lack of trust, confidence, and open emotion between David, who loved and idealized the absent mother, and Chris, and this revelation that Chris had betrayed Fran makes David as contemptuous of his father as Biff is when, in *Death of a Salesman,* he discovers Willy with the other woman in the Boston hotel room. Added to this, David must have long ago sensed that Fran and Chris had him more to bolster their "egos [that] had been wounded by [their] inability to conceive, to be the complete man and the complete woman" (242) than out of a desire to bring a child into the world and unselfishly do their best for him. But most of all, time itself is the barrier between parent and child, as it usually is in Anderson; like Roger in *Eden Rose* and Peter in *Double Solitaire,* David refuses to believe that his middle-aged father is capable of experiencing the same strong emotions that a young man feels, a problem Chris had faced as well: "I had only come to understand each phase of my father as I passed through the same phase myself" (326). In the latter instance, Marianne is, both because of the low opinion of men her mother inculcated in her and because of having at one time been sexually experimented upon by some boys, as much as castrator of Chris as Fran was. Though sex with Marianne is better than it had been "with Fran for years" (162), it simultaneously threatens to make Fran's death final by erasing her from Chris's memory. Furthermore, Marianne always holds back unless she is the dominant one in a sexual relationship: she "won't surrender [her] satisfaction completely to anyone . . . [unless she is] to a great extent in control" — unless she is, both literally and metaphorically, "on top" (259).

Yet because Marianne reminds Chris so much of Fran in her refusal to be dependent on him to satisfy her needs, he is able to confess to Fran through her that he was partly to blame for the failure of their marriage by having made her "the condition of his life" to the point where he expected she would assume the responsibility for fulfilling his life; he comes to understand that by placing this burden on her, he had, in Sartre's term, lived in "bad faith." Ultimately, like Hickey in *The Iceman Cometh,* Chris needs to tear down the mask that their marriage was perfect, to cry out, "'I *hated* her sometimes!'" (338), for he must confess his guilt before he can be judged. But while Chris acknowledges that "'we all have to learn to live guilty'" (341), unlike Gene Garrison he does not revel sentimentally in that guilt. So as Christopher Lehmann-Haupt astutely comments: "It is as if a meandering story had suddenly made up its mind to be about the illusion and reality of a marriage .... And yet for all the lumpiness of its plot and for all the artlessness of its prose, one comes to respect the integrity of this novel."[26]

Chris's self-realization and admission of guilt reveal a further growth in Anderson's attitude toward marriage, for Chris comes closer than any other of his creator's protagonists to seeing the error of idealizing and romanticizing sex. In the earlier plays (*Tea and Sympathy, Silent Night, Lonely Night*), sex outside of marriage was sanctioned for its redemptive power, while in other later ones (*I'll Be Home for Christmas, Double Solitaire*) sex inside marriage was an opportunity — perhaps the only one — for discovering meaning in a meaningless world. In *After,* sex is double-edged, with its negative aspect of being used to selfishly dominate the partner prevailing. Unlike the earlier Anderson men, Chris realizes that sex is not a panacea for every problem, that it can hurt as well as heal — something only Anderson's female characters could perceive before. And finally, Chris understands, again unlike any of Anderson's other protagonists, something else that only the women had been able to admit: that marriage is not inviolate. If Anderson points to "the preservation of a marriage" as one of his incessant themes,[27] Chris here must admit, "'If Fran weren't dying, we'd be divorced'" (286).

Whether Anderson will succeed in his second career as novelist (as this book goes to press, he has a new novel, *Getting Up and Going Home* — about marriage and separation — ready for publication early in 1978) will depend primarily on his ability to overcome the rhetorical excesses that the dramatic form, by its very nature, always helped him keep largely in check. If he does return to writing for the theater, however, any future plays undoubtedly will reflect the insights he reached in *After,* making it unlikely that any future dramas will rely on facile resolutions of the type that marred both *Silent Night, Lonely Night* or *The Days Between,* where physical intimacy is elevated into a kind of religion in the face of which all problems fade miraculously away. Rather than being an instrument to heal divisions, physical sexuality in *Double Solitaire* and *After* — whether employed as a desperate substitute for real communion between individuals, as a way of proving one's virility, or as a means of subjugating one's partner and thereby diminishing his or her selfhood — actually becomes instead the source for much of the lack of communication and loneliness within marriage.

CHAPTER 8

Conclusion

IF one excludes from consideration the "learning plays," then as Anderson himself has grown older so, too, have the protagonists of his dramas — from the preadolescent Willie in *All Summer Long* to the mid-middle-aged Charley in *Double Solitaire.* Yet, as C. W. E. Bigsby notes in his excellent brief commentary on Anderson's work, a continuity exists between the adolescents, like Willie or Tom in *Tea and Sympathy,* and the middle-aged males, like David in *The Days Between* or Charley: "the boy confronting sexuality and cruelty for the first time serves to emphasize simultaneously the ideals of youth and the cynicism and disillusionment of middle age. . . . [Anderson] see[s] growth away from innocence into experience as the first stage in the extinction of genuine feeling and human compassion. If some people can sustain their innocence into maturity they do so, in his world it seems, only at the cost of their ability to act."[1] What causes the loneliness and disillusionment that pervade the world of Anderson's plays is, put simply, the tendency of American society not only to undervalue sensitivity but, whenever possible, to destroy it, as part of perpetuating a distorted notion of manliness.

America is, as Anderson implies through Tom Garrison, whose life becomes a microcosm of the nation's history in *I Never Sang for My Father* (a drama that is, finally, as much about America as Arthur Miller's *Death of a Salesman* is), a country built on the "masculine" virtues of self-reliance and aggressiveness, on the lust for power and material success. So this New World, inherently incomplete and unbalanced because it lacks the "feminine" spirit of gentleness and kindness and compassion, could never be Eden regained; it was doomed to be a paradise lost from the very beginning. The closest that any of Anderson's characters come to recapturing an idyllic existence is at the end of his unproduced original filmscript, *A Small Part of a Long Story.* And it is nearly reached there precisely because both Jeff Bridger and his wife Kit balance within themselves masculine strength and assertiveness with feminine tenderness and sensibility and are thus able to fuse love with sex; Jeff, vulnerable because of his physical sterility, is still man enough to allow Kit to be temporarily the stronger half of the partnership.

The loss of innocence and disillusionment that Anderson's characters undergo begins not when they are thrust into the imperfect world outside, but usually within the family itself. For his adolescents like Willie or Tom or Roger in *Days Between* it begins with fathers who fear any open display of emotion with their sons — since this would reveal an unmanly weakness —, who are embarrassed to tell their sons about sex and, in fact, cannot, because they know so little of love, and who insist that the sons do something to make the fathers proud of them; this last ordinarily entails attempting to snuff out any "difference" in the direction of sensitivity, like the love of music and writing exhibited by Tom in *Tea and Sympathy* or by Gene Garrison in *I Never Sang for My Father.* So the fathers in Anderson, because they do nothing positive to compensate for the gulf that time inevitably wedges between parent and child, are — with the possible exception of Charley in *Double Solitaire* — failures as fathers, though they seldom experience any guilt over this.

They are, nevertheless, often disillusioned by other things. It might be, as for Gene in *I Never Sang for My Father,* by their own failure as a son. Or it might be by the "intimations" of their own mortality, or by their sense that the old value systems have disintegrated around them (John Sparrow in *Silent Night, Lonely Night,* Chuck in *I'll Be Home for Christmas*); and for some reason the men seem less capable of living with values in flux than do women like Laura in *Tea and Sympathy* or Katherine in *Silent Night,* who can eventually set aside or adjust their traditional ethical strictures in favor of a higher morality of responding to another person in a situation of need. Or the Anderson males might also be frightened by their awareness of compromised goals and unfulfilled dreams, which could lead to cynicism and a defeatist retreat from life (John Bosworth in *Come Marching Home,* Charles Webster in *Love Revisited*, Don in *All Summer Long,* David in *Days Between*), or by their recognition of diminishing possibilities with the passage of time, of fewer roads left to travel and fewer choices left to make as they draw closer to death (especially true of Charley in *Double Solitaire*). And these anxieties, some more tangible than others, often come not singly, but converge all at once, so that middle age becomes as traumatic a time as adolescence had been.

But mostly these middle-aged men are disillusioned by the waning of sex within marriage, the very thing that they count on to prove their vitality and to provide a cushion for warding off the existential void. But this is a bind in which they have placed themselves by their adolescent obsession with sex as a means of proving their masculinity, and by their immature tendency to romanticize and idealize sex into a panacea for all their ills. In Anderson's early and middle plays — from *Come Marching Home* through *The Days Between* — there is a discernible tendency among the protagonists, as well as on the part of the dramatist himself, to worship mothers and surrogate mothers (Nan Hilton in *The Eden Rose,* Laura in *Tea and Sympathy*), lovers (again Laura, as well as Katherine in *Silent Night*), and wives and surrogate wives (once more Katherine, together with Toni Bosworth in *Marching Home* and Barbara in *Days Between*). Sometimes Anderson's sympathies and point of view are so closely allied with the emotionally starved females, particularly Barbara in *Days Between,* who is little more than an appendage of her husband, that one is even tempted to categorize Anderson as a feminist playwright; certainly, with the exception of William Inge, he is the only dramatist of his generation to probe incessantly the male-female relationship within marriage.

But in Anderson's later plays, as if to redress this perhaps excessive idealization of women, it is not the women themselves who are venerated, but rather physical sexuality, even at the risk of reducing women merely to objects, which the protagonists idealize — and that at the very time when such wives as Harriet in *The Footsteps of Doves* or Barbara in *Double Solitaire,* whose husbands are more in love with the idea of sex than with the women they married, crave some means of communication other than physical intimacy. Finally, in the novel *After,* both the protagonist and Anderson himself understand that these idealizations of women as wives and lovers, of marriage as an inviolate union of eternal happiness, and of physical sexuality as an experience of almost mystic proportions have in themselves been destructive and caused the very loneliness and disillusionment they were designed to guard against.

Though Anderson may seem to repeat the same plot over and over again, *After,* with its ambivalent love-hate relationship, indicates that his attitudes have matured and his insights deepened along with those of his protagonists. One limitation on the range and variety of his work has perhaps been the autobiographical stimulus itself (he has said, "Every play I've ever written is me. I am naked when I finish"[2]) that appears to have kept his imagination in check. Yet if the subject matter is repetitious, his structure, style, and tone vary significantly: from the well-made play, *Come Marching Home,* to the morality play, *Double Solitaire;* from the setting designed to create the illusion of reality in *Silent Night, Lonely Night* to the nonrepresentational narrative form of *I Never Sang for My Father;* from the near tragedy of *Tea and Sympathy* to the farcical comedy of *I'm Herbert;* from the philosophical pessimism of *All Summer Long* to the tempered optimism of *A Small Part of a Long Story.* Despite Anderson's tendencies toward rhetorical excess, to telling rather than dramatizing, to allowing sentiment to spill over into sentimentality, he does exhibit one consistent strength; as Peter says of his father's work in *Double Solitaire:* "What's real in these stories . . . is the ache and longing and pain."[3]

In a remark that one could imagine Anderson someday choosing for his epitaph, John Gassner, who nurtured Anderson's career from its beginning, called him "a gentleman in the age of literary assassins."[4] Fashions have changed in the theater as in everything else, and gentlemanly Anderson may seem more a playwright for the placid fifties and early sixties than for the turbulent late sixties and seventies, when audiences are accustomed to being assaulted both verbally and visually by such impressive dramas as David Rabe's *The Basic Training of Pavlo Hummel* and *Sticks and Bones.* And yet one feels confident that Robert Anderson's plays will remain popular, not only because audiences can find in them discussions similar to those in the best-selling books by sociologists and psychologists and sexologists that clinically diagnose man's emotional disorders and sexual problems, but most especially because of Anderson's humanity and compassion in portraying his distraught and lonely creatures. This last virtue is one in which, among Anderson's contemporaries, only Tennessee Williams can equal or surpass him.

Notes and References

Chapter One

1. *I Never Sang for My Father* (New York, 1968), p. 3.
2. *Ibid.,* p. 113.
3. "The Arts Around Us" (Taped interview with Elizabeth Karp), March 21, 1973.
4. David H. Ayers, "The Apprenticeship of Robert Anderson" (Dissertation, Ohio State University, 1969), p. 17.
5. "Maxwell Anderson: An Appreciation," *The American Film Theater/Cinebill,* 1, viii (January 1974), unpaged.
6. For a thorough discussion of these college plays, see Ayers, pp. 23–41, whose summaries are the basis for the comments that follow.
7. Ayers, p. 32.
8. *Tea and Sympathy* (New York, 1953), p. v.
9. Lawrence Langer et al., "This Is for Phyllis," *Theater Arts,* 41, iv (April 1957), 81. For an extended appreciative portrait of Phyllis Anderson, see Arthur Cavanaugh, *My Own Back Yard* (Garden City, N.Y., 1962), pp. 141–238.
10. John F. Wharton, *Life Among the Playwrights: Being Mostly the Story of The Playwrights Producing Company* (New York, 1974), p. 241.
11. Robert Anderson in a letter to the author, May 14, 1974.
12. *Ibid.*
13. Robert Anderson, Untitled article on the New Dramatists Committee (1960 typescript in the Theater Collection of the New York Public Library for the Performing Arts at Lincoln Center).
14. Norman Nadel, *A Pictorial History of the Theatre Guild* (New York, 1969), p. 214.
15. Roy S. Waldau, *Vintage Years of the Theatre Guild: 1928–1939* (Cleveland, Ohio, 1972), p. 388.
16. Recorded transcripts of twenty-five of these adaptations are housed in the Yale Collection of Historical Sound Recordings.
17. Letter to the author, April 22, 1974.
18. Ayers, pp. 88–89.
19. Letter to the author, April 22, 1974.
20. "No Final Curtain on the Ghosts of Grief," *Prism,* August 1974, p. 50.

21. *Ibid.,* p. 53.
22. *Ibid.,* p. 50.
23. Wharton, pp. 242–44.
24. George Middleton, *The Dramatists Guild* (New York, 1966), p. 18.
25. "Draw Your Own Conclusions," *Theatre Arts,* 38, ix (September 1954), 32.
26. "Thoughts on Playwriting," *Writer,* 83, ix (September 1970), 13.
27. "The Playwright and His Craft," *Writer,* 68, v (May 1955), 154.
28. "Writing for Performance" (First Marvin Borowsky Memorial Lecture, Academy of Motion Picture Arts and Sciences, Los Angeles, April 29, 1974), p. 59.
29. "Thoughts on Playwriting," p. 14.
30. "The Playwright in the Modern Theatre" (1956 typescript in the Theater Collection at Lincoln Center).
31. "Thoughts on Playwriting," p. 13.
32. "The Playwright: Man and Mission," *Theatre Arts,* 42, iii (March 1958), 49.
33. "Walk a Ways With Me," *Theatre Arts,* 38, i (January 1954), 30.
34. "The Playwright in the Modern Theatre."
35. "'Every Play I've Ever Written Is Me. I Am Naked When I Finish.': A Conversation" (with Janet Baker-Carr), *Harvard Magazine,* 77, viii (April 1975), 41.
36. "Robert Anderson — An Interview" (with Patricia Bosworth), *Publisher's Weekly,* ii July 9, 1973, p. 17.
37. "Portrait in Playwriting" (Tape of video telecast for WOSU-TV), July 28, 1966.
38. *After* (New York, 1973), p. 265.
39. "'Every Play I've Ever Written is Me,'" p. 42.
40. J. Chesley Taylor and G. R. Thompson, eds., *Ritual, Realism and Revolt: Major Traditions in the Drama* (New York, 1972), p. 544.
41. "Writing for Performance," p. 24.
42. "Portrait in Playwriting."
43. Gerald Weales, *The Jumping-Off Place: American Drama in the 1960's* (New York, 1969), p. 228.
44. "Interview (Bosworth)," p. 16.
45. Robert Brustein, *Seasons of Discontent: Dramatic Opinions 1959–1965* (New York, 1965), p. 284.
46. "Forum's Pair of One-Acters: Two Kinds of Loneliness," *Chicago Sun-Times,* July 21, 1974, sec. III, p. 2.
47. "Toward a Semiotic Theory of the Drama," *Educational Theatre Journal,* 26 (December 1974), 453–54.
48. Conversation with the author, June 4, 1974.

Chapter Two

1. Interview with the author, June 4, 1974.
2. Letter to the author, April 18, 1974.
3. *The New York Times,* May 20, 1946, p. 18.
4. *The Theatre Book of the Year 1946-47: A Record and an Interpretation* (New York, 1947), p. 25.
5. Interview, June 4, 1974.
6. Nathan, p. 26.
7. *Come Marching Home* (Unpublished play). References will be cited by act, scene, and page number within the text.
8. William F. Bottiglia, "Candide's Garden," in *Voltaire: A Collection of Critical Essays,* ed. William F. Bottiglia (Englewood Cliffs, N.J., 1968), p. 91.
9. Henrik Ibsen, *An Enemy of the People,* in *Collected Works of Ibsen* (New York, undated), p. 139. See Michael Meyer, *Ibsen: A Biography* (Garden City, N.Y., 1971), p. 507, for comparison with Mill.
10. *The Eden Rose* (Unpublished play). References will be cited by act and page number within the text.
11. Philip Barry, *Paris Bound* (New York, 1929), pp. 19, 22.
12. Eugene O'Neill, *Strange Interlude,* in *Nine Plays* (New York, 1932), p. 669.
13. Eugene O'Neill, *Ah, Wilderness!,* in *The Later Plays of Eugene O'Neill,* ed. Travis Bogard (New York, 1967), p. 130.
14. Booth Tarkington, *The Magnificent Ambersons* (New York, 1960), p. 31.
15. Inge was so impressed with Anderson's suggestions for *Come Back, Little Sheba* that he later asked Anderson to collaborate with him on an early version of the play that eventually became the Pulitzer Prize winning *Picnic,* but Anderson refused because he thought their styles were "too dissimilar." (Interview, June 4, 1974).
16. Interview, June 4, 1974.
17. Ayers, p. 39.
18. *Solitaire/Double Solitaire* (New York, 1972), p. 39.
19. *Love Revisited* (Unpublished play). References will be cited by act and page number within the text.

Chapter Three

1. Interview, June 4, 1974.
2. Donald Wetzel, *A Wreath and a Curse* (New York, 1950). Page references appear within the text.
3. Anderson will employ a similar imagistic pattern of the human

reduced to the animal very extensively in his unproduced original filmscript, *A Small Part of a Long Story* (1962).

4. Feike Feikema, *Chicago Sun-Times,* January 31, 1950, p. 55.

5. *All Summer Long* (New York, 1955). Page references are cited within the text.

6. "A Postscript ... Not a Post-Mortem," *Theatre Arts,* 39, viii (August 1955), 33.

7. Tom Donnelly, "Something in Willie Loved a Wall," *Women's Wear Daily,* January 15, 1953, p. 19, and *Women's Wear Daily,* September 7, 1954, p. 44; Jay Carmody, "Touching Play of Boyhood Opens National Season," *The Evening Star* (Washington, D.C.), September 7, 1954, p. 29.

8. Richard Coe, "Gentle Play Opens National's Season," *The Washington Post-Herald,* September 8, 1954, p. 38.

9. Richard Coe, "A Hit Play's Uphill Trek," *The Washington Post-Herald,* September 12, 1954, p. 36.

10. Brooks Atkinson, *"All Summer Long," The New York Times,* October 3, 1954, sec. 2, p. 1.

11. Brooks Atkinson, "Theatre: Coming of Age," *The New York Times,* September 24, 1954, p. 39; and Atkinson, *Times,* October 3, 1954, sec. 2, p. 1.

12. W. David Sievers, *Freud on Broadway: A History of Psychoanalysis and the American Drama* (New York, 1955), p. 411.

13. Atkinson, *Times,* October 3, 1954, sec. 2, p. 1.

14. Brooks Atkinson, "Forward," *New Voices in the American Theatre* (New York, 1955), p. xi.

15. Interview, June 4, 1974.

16. John Van Druten, *Young Woodley* (New York, 1930). Page references appear within the text.

17. Ayers, p. 133. Ayers's summaries of this short story and of the novel *Birthright,* also unpublished, again serve as the basis for the discussion here.

18. "Some Notes on *Tea and Sympathy,*" *The Exonian,* 224, xiv (March 3, 1954), p. 14.

19. "Draw Your Own Conclusions," ix, p. 33.

20. Ayers, p. 141.

21. "Person to Person," *Cat on a Hot Tin Roof* (New York, 1955), p. ix.

22. "Some Notes on *Tea and Sympathy,*" pp. 14–15.

23. *Ibid.,* p. 15.

24. Untitled comment in *Contemporary Dramatists,* ed. James Vinson (London, 1973), p. 33. Several critics perceive this theme, among them John Gassner, *Best American Plays: Fourth Series — 1951–57* (New York, 1958), p. xviii.

25. Page references for *Tea and Sympathy* appear within the text.

26. "Some Notes on *Tea and Sympathy,*" p. 16.
27. *Ibid.*
28. Sievers, p. 411; and John Gassner, *Theatre at the Crossroads: Plays and Playwrights of the Mid-Century American Stage* (New York, 1960), p. 292.
29. Gerald Weales, *American Drama Since World War II* (New York, 1962), pp. 49–50; Henry Hewes, "Broadway Postscript: Orange Pekoe," *The Saturday Review,* 36 (October 17, 1953), 35.
30. Untitled comment, *Dramatists,* p. 33.
31. Quoted in Vincente Minnelli, *I Remember It Well* (New York, 1975), p. 311.
32. Eric Bentley, *The Dramatic Event: An American Chronicle* (New York, 1954), p. 152.
33. Tennessee Williams, *A Streetcar Named Desire* (New York, 1947), p. 96.
34. Williams, *Cat,* p. 158.
35. Sievers, p. 411.
36. Walter Kerr, *How Not to Write a Play* (New York, 1955), pp. 108–10.
37. "Notes on *Tea and Sympathy,*" p. 15.
38. Murray Schumach, *The Face on the Cutting Room Floor: The Story of Movie and Television Censorship* (New York, 1974), p. 144.
39. Erwin Panofsky, "Style and Medium in the Motion Pictures," in *Film Theory and Criticism,* ed. Gerald Mast and Marshall Cohen (New York, 1974), pp. 154–55. Recently, however, Stanley Kauffmann has argued that "In good [theater productions], the eye has very little more choice than at a film." "On Theater," *New Republic,* August 16, 23, 1975, p. 41.
40. *Tea and Sympathy* (Unpublished filmscript). Page references will be cited within the text.
41. Ayers comments on Anderson's use of flower symbolism, pp. 71–72.
42. A. R. Fulton, *Motion Pictures: The Development of an Art* (Norman, Okla., 1960), p. 276.
43. Bosley Crowther, *"Tea and Sympathy," New York Times,* September 28, 1956, p. 24.
44. Hollis Alpert, "What Hangs Over," *Saturday Review,* September 29, 1956, p. 31.

Chapter Four

1. "Writing for Performance," p. 9.
2. Interview, June 4, 1974.
3. "Writing for Performance," pp. 14, 25.

4. The question of whether a filmscript constitutes literature continues to be debated. Although as far back as 1943, John Gassner wrote that "'there is now a literature of the screen . . . . film writing already has substantial claims to literary recognition,'" more recently Hollis Alpert has said: "But whether final shooting scripts should be regarded as literature is still a dubious proposition. That some scripts have literary *quality* is undeniable." Alpert, "But Who Wrote the Movie?" *Saturday Review,* December 26, 1970, p. 9.

5. James A. Michener, *Return to Paradise* (New York, 1951), p. 437.

6. *Ibid.,* p. 267.

7. *Until They Sail* (Unpublished filmscript). Page references appear within the text.

8. Michener, p. 273.

9. Bosley Crowther, *"Until They Sail," New York Times,* October 9, 1957, p. 41.

10. Interview, June 4, 1974.

11. Neil P. Hurley, *Toward a Film Humanism* (New York, 1975), pp. 59, 70.

12. *The Nun's Story* (Unpublished filmscript). Page references appear within the text.

13. Kathryn Hulme, *The Nun's Story* (New York, 1956), pp. 255-56.

14. Stanley Kauffmann, *A World on Film: Criticism and Comment* (New York, 1951), p. 50; Arthur Knight, "The World and the Spirit," *Saturday Review,* June 27, 1959, 24.

15. Harold Toliver, *Animate Illusions: Explorations of Narrative* (Lincoln, Neb., 1974), p. 197.

16. Interview, June 4, 1974.

17. *A Small Part of a Long Story* (Unpublished filmscript). Page references appear within the text.

18. Anderson has said that Phyllis's "career was my child, and my career was her child." Interview, June 4, 1974.

19. Interview, June 4, 1974.

20. Arthur Knight, "Unsentimental Gentleman," *Saturday Review,* December 24, 1966, p. 62.

21. "Writing for Performance," p. 27.

22. Robert Wise, "Dialogue on Film," *American Film,* 1, ii (November 1975), 39.

23. George Bluestone, *Novels Into Film: The Metamorphosis of Fiction Into Cinema* (Berkeley, Calif., 1971), p. 62.

24. *The Sand Pebbles* (Unpublished filmscript). Page references appear within the text.

25. John P. Sisk, "Hot Sporting Blood," *Commonweal,* March 2, 1973, 496.

26. John Gassner, *Best American Plays: Fifth Series — 1957–63* (New York, 1963), p. 314.

Chapter Five

1. Untitled comment in *Contemporary Dramatists,* pp. 32–33.
2. Wharton, p. 27.
3. Untitled reminiscence of The Playwrights Company (1954 typescript in the Theater Collection at Lincoln Center).
4. *Ibid.*
5. Wharton, pp. 248, 263.
6. Gassner, *Best American Plays: Fifth Series — 1957–63,* p. 314.
7. "Thoughts on Playwriting," p. 14.
8. "Introduction to *Silent Night, Lonely Night,*" *Theatre Arts,* 45, xii (December 1961), 26.
9. Weales, *American Drama Since World War II,* p. 51.
10. *Silent Night, Lonely Night* (New York, 1960). Page references appear within the text.
11. "The Arts Around Us."
12. Allan Lewis, *American Plays and Playwrights of the Contemporary Theatre* (New York, 1970), p. 155.
13. *Solitaire/Double Solitaire* (New York, 1972), p. 65.
14. Letter to the author, August 7, 1975.
15. Jerome Lawrence and Robert E. Lee, "111 Productions of a New Play On the 'New Broadway' Circuit," *Dramatists Guild Quarterly,* 8, ii (Summer 1971), 5.
16. *Ibid.,* p. 8.
17. *Ibid.,* pp. 5–6.
18. "APT: Here's a Chance for Playwrights to Work in a More Stable Theater," *Dramatists Guild Quarterly,* 4, ii (Summer 1967), 5.
19. *Ibid.,* p. 6.
20. Taped interview with Gene Gerard, Columbus, Ohio, July 8, 1966.
21. *The Days Between,* revised version (New York, 1969). Page references appear within the text.
22. David H. Ayers comments on the multiple levels required by Anderson's set descriptions for the plays up through *Tea and Sympathy,* pp. 154–55.
23. Ayers, p. 206.
24. Vivien Leone, "Notes from an Accidentally Passionate Playgoer," *Drama & Theatre,* 10, iii (Spring 1972), 136.
25. Langer, iv p. 80, as reported by Elia Kazan.
26. *The Days Between* (New York, 1965), p. 120.
27. "*Days Between* Bows in Dallas Center," *New York Times,* June 4, 1965, p. 39.

28. Interview, June 4, 1974.

Chapter Six

1. Ayers, p. 223.
2. *Ibid.*, p. 222.
3. Stephen Marcus, *London Sunday Telegraph,* June 30, 1968, p. 12.
4. Untitled comment, *Contemporary Dramatists,* p. 33.
5. John Simon, *Uneasy Stages: A Chronicle of the New York Theater 1963–1973* (New York, 1975), p. 109; Roderick Nordell, *Christian Science Monitor,* March 13, 1968, p. 10.
6. Ayers, p. 110.
7. Walter Kerr, *God on the Gymnasium Floor and Other Theatrical Adventures* (New York, 1973), p. 105.
8. *You Know I Can't Hear You When the Water's Running* (New York, 1967). Page references appear within the text.
9. Kerr, *God on the Gymnasium Floor,* p. 106.
10. John Lahr, *Up Against the Fourth Wall: Essays on Modern Theatre* (New York, 1970), pp. 7–8.
11. "Portrait in Playwriting."
12. Letter, January 22, 1975.
13. Interview, June 4, 1974.
14. Quoted in Martin Esslin, *The Theatre of the Absurd* (New York, 1961), p. xix.
15. Ayers, p. 228.
16. Gilbert Cates, "Notes on Making the Film," in *I Never Sang For My Father* — Filmscript (New York, 1970), p. 19.
17. Frank Marcus, *London Sunday Telegraph,* May 31, 1970, p. 14; and Irving Wardle, *London Times,* May 28, 1970, p. 16.
18. *I Never Sang for My Father*. Page references appear within the text.
19. "Introduction," *I Never Sang for My Father* — Filmscript, p. 13.
20. Interview, June 4, 1974.
21. Ayers, p. 5. Anderson now says "No one sees that play" (Interview, June 4, 1974).
22. Henry Hewes, "The Best of the 1967–68 Theater Season," *Saturday Review,* June 1, 1968, p. 13.
23. Interview, June 4, 1974.
24. *Ibid.*
25. Joseph McBride, *Orson Welles* (New York, 1972), p. 11.
26. Robert Heilman, *The Iceman, the Arsonist, and the Troubled Agent: Tragedy and Melodrama on the Modern Stage* (Seattle, 1973), p. 33.
27. Anderson, "Introduction," *I Never Sang for My Father,* p. 13.

28. Rex Reed, "Melvin Douglas Not Ruffled by Awards or Age," *Chicago Tribune,* January 17, 1971, 5, p. 1.

29. Edward Anhalt, *The Screenwriter Looks at the Screenwriter,* ed. William Fronz (New York, 1972), p. 260.

30. *I Never Sang for My Father* — Filmscript, p. 158. Page references appear within the text.

31. Tennessee Williams, *The Glass Menagerie* (New York, 1966), pp. 114–15.

32. For a telling contrast, see the sequence in which Harry visits Jessie in the nursing home in Paul Mazursky's 1973 film, *Harry and Tonto.*

33. Robert Jay Lifton and Eric Olson, *Living and Dying* (New York, 1974), p. 46.

34. Edward Murray, *The Cinematic Imagination: Writers and the Motion Picture* (New York, 1972), p. 14.

35. Cates, p. 19.

Chapter Seven

1. Winifred L. Dusenbury, *The Theme of Loneliness in Modern American Drama* (Gainesville, Fla., 1960), p. 5.

2. *"Forum's Pair of One-Acters: Two Kinds of Loneliness,"* p. 2.

3. *After.* Page references appear within the text.

4. *Solitaire/Double Solitaire.* Page references appear within the text.

5. Julius Novick also suggests this comparison. "On the Road to Dystopia," *Village Voice,* October 7, 1971, p. 52.

6. Interview, June 4, 1974.

7. Catharine Hughes, *Solitaire/Double Solitaire, America,* October 23, 1971, p. 322.

8. Henry Hewes, "A Husband's Undoing," *Saturday Review,* October 16, 1971, p. 35; and George Birrell, *Edinburgh Evening News,* September 7, 1971, p. 19.

9. Interview, June 4, 1974.

10. Walter Kerr, *The Silent Clowns* (New York, 1975), pp. 3–4.

11. Richard Watts, "A Symposium on Marriage," *New York Post,* October 1, 1971, p. 29.

12. Martin Gottfried, *Women's Wear Daily,* October 1, 1971, p. 11.

13. Leone, p. 134.

14. Douglas Watt, "Two Anderson Playlets (Ho-Hum) Open Broadway Season," *Daily News,* October 1, 1971, p. 68.

15. The phrase is John F. Crosby's in *Illusion and Disillusion: The Self in Love and Marriage* (Belmont, Calif., 1973), p. 1.

16. Letter, September 9, 1974.

17. Letter, January 22, 1975.

18. Richard Kerckhoff coined this designation in an address before the Indiana Council on Family Relations, February 1974.

19. Elia Kazan, *The Understudy* (New York, 1976), p. 219.

20. Handwritten inscription in this author's copy of *Solitaire/Double Solitaire,* inscribed June 4, 1974.

21. Interview, June 4, 1974.

22. Ayers, p. 187.

23. Interview (with Patricia Bosworth), p. 16.

24. "No Final Curtain on the Ghosts of Grief," p. 53.

25. "Interview (Bosworth)," p. 16.

26. Christopher Lehmann-Haupt, "Connections, Disconnections," *New York Times,* July 5, 1973, p. 27.

27. Letter, September 9, 1974.

Chapter Eight

1. C. W. E. Bigsby, Untitled commentary, *Contemporary Dramatists,* ed. James Vinson (London, 1973), p. 35.

2. "'Every Play I've Ever Written Is Me,'" p. 41.

3. *Solitaire/Double Solitaire,* p. 65.

4. Gassner, *Best American Plays: Fifth Series — 1957-63,* p. 314.

Selected Bibliography

PRIMARY SOURCES

1. Major works by Robert Anderson (Plays unless otherwise noted)

After (Novel). New York: Random House, 1973.
All Summer Long, New York: Samuel French, Inc., 1955.
Come Marching Home. Unpublished play, 1945.
The Days Between. New York: Random House, 1965.
The Days Between. Revised version. New York: Samuel French, Inc., 1969.
The Eden Rose. Unpublished play, 1948.
I Never Sang for My Father. New York: Random House, 1968.
I Never Sang for My Father (Filmscript). New York: New American Library, 1970.
Love Revisited. Unpublished play, 1951.
The Nun's Story. Unpublished filmscript, 1959.
The Sand Pebbles. Unpublished filmscript, 1966.
Silent Night, Lonely Night. New York: Random House, 1960.
A Small Part of a Long Story. Unpublished original filmscript, 1962.
Solitaire/Double Solitaire. New York: Random House, 1972.
Tea and Sympathy. New York: Random House, 1953.
Until They Sail. Unpublished filmscript, 1957.
You Know I Can't Hear You When the Water's Running. New York: Random House, 1967.

2. Robert Anderson's essays, lectures, and interviews

"APT: Here's a Chance for Playwrights to Work in a More Stable Theater." *Dramatists Guild Quarterly,* 4, ii (Spring 1967), 4–8. Reprinted as "American Playwrights Theater: More than Fifty Productions Coast to Coast." In *The Best Plays of 1966–67,* ed. Otis L. Guernsey, Jr., pp. 49–53. New York: Dodd, Mead & Company, 1967.
"The Arts Around Us." Taped interview with Elizabeth Karp, New York, March 21, 1973.

"Drama Mailbag: Who's to Blame? The Albee Debate." *New York Times,* April 25, 1965, p. 4.

"Draw Your Own Conclusions," *Theatre Arts,* 38, ix, 32–33.

"'Every Play I've Ever Written Is Me. I Am Naked When I Finish': A Conversation" (with Janet Baker-Carr). *Harvard Magazine,* 77, viii (April 1975), 40–45.

"Forum's Pair of One-Acters: Two Kinds of Loneliness." *Chicago Sun-Times,* July 21, 1974, sec. III, p. 2.

"Interview with American Academy of Dramatic Arts" (for WNTA-TV). New York, January 14, 1961.

"Introduction to *I Never Sang for My Father.*" In *The Best Plays of 1967–68,* ed. Otis L. Guernsey, Jr. pp. 278–80. New York: Dodd, Mead & Company, 1968.

"Introduction." *I Never Sang for My Father* (filmscript), pp. 9–13. New York: New American Library, 1970.

"Introduction to *Silent Night, Lonely Night.*" *Theatre Arts,* 45, xii (December 1961), 26.

"Maxwell Anderson: An Appreciation." *The American Film Theatre/ Cinebill,* 1, viii (January 1974), unpaged.

"No Final Curtain on the Ghosts of Grief." *Prism,* August 1974, pp. 50–53.

"Notes to APT Producers." Included in 1965 mimeographed production scripts of *The Days Between.*

"A Playwright Talks to Us." *The Cue* (Indiana State University), 30, iii (Spring 1955), 2–3.

"The Playwright and His Craft." *Writer,* 68, v (May 1955), 152–54.

"The Playwright: Man and Mission." *Theatre Arts,* 42, iii (March 1958), 49.

"The Playwright in the Modern Theatre." Unpublished 1956 typescript in the Theater Collection of the New York Library for the Performing Arts at Lincoln Center.

"Portrait in Playwriting." Videotape of telecast for WOSU-TV, Columbus, Ohio, July 28, 1966.

"A Postscript . . . Not a Post-Mortem." *Theatre Arts,* 39, viii (August 1955), 32–33.

"Robert Anderson." Taped interview with Gene Gerard, Columbus, Ohio, July 8, 1966.

"Robert Anderson — An Interview" (with Patricia Bosworth). *Publisher's Weekly,* July 9, 1973, pp. 16–17.

"Recent Study of Broadway Theatre is Welcome, but Too Optimistic." *Dramatists Guild Quarterly,* 9, i (Spring 1972), 6, 10–11.

"Some Notes on *Tea and Sympathy.*" *The Exonian* (Phillips Exeter Academy), 224, xiv (March 3, 1954), 14–16.

"The Theatre is Such an Impossible Place, Maybe It's Only Meant for Miracles." *Dramatists Guild Quarterly,* 2, i (Spring 1965), 3–5.

"Thoughts on Playwriting." *Writer,* 83, ix (September 1970), 12–14.

Untitled article on the New Dramatists Committee. 1960 typescript in the Theater Collection at Lincoln Center.

Untitled comment. In *Contemporary Dramatists,* ed. James Vinson, pp. 32–33. London: St. James Press, 1973.

Untitled homage to Elia Kazan. In *Working with Kazan* (published on the Occasion of a Complete Retrospective of the Films of Elia Kazan), ed. Jeanine Basinger, John Frazer, and Joseph W. Reed, Jr. Middleton, Conn.: Wesleyan University Press, 1973. unpaged.

Untitled reminiscence of The Playwrights Company. 1954 typescript in the Theater Collection at Lincoln Center.

"Walk a Ways With Me." *Theatre Arts,* 38, i (January 1954), 30–31.

"Writing for Performance." Typed copy of the First Marvin Borowsky Memorial Lecture, Academy of Motion Picture Arts and Sciences, Los Angeles, California, April 29, 1974. 60 pp.

SECONDARY SOURCES

ADLER, THOMAS P. "Robert Anderson: Playwright of Middle-Aged Loneliness." *Ball State University Forum,* 16, ii (Spring 1975), 58–64. A short study of the produced plays that is the genesis of this book.

AYERS, DAVID H. "The Apprenticeship of Robert Anderson." Dissertation, Ohio State University, 1969. A "professional biography," particularly useful for its information on Anderson's life and unpublished works as well as his critical reception.

BENTLEY, ERIC. *The Dramatic Event: An American Chronicle.* New York: Horizon Press, 1954. Pp. 150–52. Discusses *Tea and Sympathy* as "a highly superior specimen of the theatre of 'realist' escape."

BIGSBY, C. W. E. Untitled commentary, in *Contemporary Dramatists,* ed. James Vinson, pp. 34–36. London: St. James Press, 1973. The best capsule assessment of Anderson's work, pointing to his tendency toward "dramatic overstatement" but concluding that he is often "a writer of genuine power and considerable subtlety."

GASSNER, JOHN. *Theatre at the Crossroads: Plays and Playwrights of the Mid-Century American Stage.* New York: Holt, Rinehart & Winston, 1960. Pp. 288–94. A generally favorable analysis of Anderson's work by his chief critical apologist, who prizes his "sensitivity .... feeling and insight."

HERRON, IMA HONAKER. *The Small Town in American Drama.* Dallas: Southern Methodist University Press, 1969. Pp. 457–65. Good brief analyses, focusing on character and theme, of Anderson's four major plays up to 1965, emphasizing "Anderson's rare talent for dramatizing lonely townspeople."

KERR, WALTER. *How Not to Write a Play.* New York: Simon & Schuster, 1955. Pp. 108–11. Considers *Tea and Sympathy* as a highly successful example of the "well-made formula," which inevitably "takes a certain toll of honesty, accuracy, and unfettered observation."

LEONE, VIVIEN. "Notes From an Accidentally Passionate Playgoer." *Drama & Theatre,* 10, iii (Spring 1972), 134–36. A review essay on *Solitaire/Double Solitaire* expressing great delight over the discovery that Anderson espouses a feminist viewpoint.

MESERVE, WALTER J. *An Outline History of American Drama.* Totowa, N.J.: Littlefield, Adams & Co., 1965. Pp. 351–52. A necessarily short comment on Anderson as a writer of sentimental comedies and melodramas marred by their "slow movement" and Anderson's "unrelenting emphasis on sweetness, sentiment, and illicit sex as a solution to man's problems."

WEALES, GERALD. *American Drama Since World War II.* New York: Harcourt, Brace & World, Inc., 1962. Pp. 49–56. A negative critique of Anderson's work, castigating the sentimentality and melodrama that have gained him a "reputation for seriousness."

WHARTON, JAMES F. *Life Among the Playwrights: Being Mostly the Story of The Playwrights Producing Company.* New York: Quadrangle/New York Times Book Company, 1974. Pp. 237–51. Recounts Anderson's association with one of the most illustrious producers of drama in America.

Index

(The works of Anderson are listed under his name)

Actor's Studio, The, 20
Adler, Richard, 22
After the Fall (Miller), 27
Ah, Wilderness! (O'Neill), 24, 40
Alger, Horatio, 138
All About Eve, 159
All My Sons (Miller), 34
American Dream, The (Albee), 63
American Playwrights Theater, The, 22, 112-13
American Theater Wing, The, 20
Anderson, Maxwell, 16-17, 18, 20, 102, 103
Anderson, Robert: as comedy of manners dramatist, 18, 21, 45, 52; as nonrepresentational playwright, 23, 135, 148-49; as practitioner of well-made play, 23, 24, 30, 33, 43, 45, 120; as teacher, 17, 20, 22-23; as writer of filmscripts, 21, 22, 81-85, 86-101, 141-44; biography of, 15-23; disillusionment as theme in, 30, 33, 36, 49, 90, 107, 116, 164, 165-66; double plot in, 41, 107, 116, 153; education of, 15, 16, 17, 19; father-son relationships in, 34, 59, 61-62, 73, 134, 136-37, 139-41, 152, 159-60; loneliness as theme in, 42, 72, 79, 87, 88, 89, 100, 104-106, 108, 112, 145-48, 150, 162, 165; loss of wife as subject in, 18, 109, 136, 139, 146, 155-57, 160; marriage as subject in, 18, 19, 45-47, 50-52, 59, 63-64, 75, 76, 79, 80, 85, 94-97, 105-106, 111, 116, 119-20, 121, 127-29, 131, 149-55, 158, 165; marriages of, 18-19, 21, 22; middle-age as a concern in, 45-46, 49, 65, 107, 115, 118-19, 130-32, 142-43, 154, 165; mother-son relationships in, 34-5, 59, 64, 136-37, 139, 140, 165; Navy service of, 17, 19; on men as romantics in sex, 40, 42, 51, 116, 126, 128, 143, 150, 151, 152-53, 161, 165; stage symbols in, 45, 51, 60, 67, 110, 116, 127; situation etics in, 77, 78-79, 87, 104, 106, 108-111; time as theme in, 39, 44-45, 46-47, 132-34; writer-characters in, 15, 19, 25, 30, 48-50, 52, 107, 115-18, 121

WORKS—DRAMA:

All Summer Long, 18, 21, 46, 49, 54, *58-69*, 73, 75, 90, 92, 102, 104, 115, 129, 130, 131, 134, 139, 147, 163, 164, 166
Anthony Babington, 18
Boy Grown Tall, 19
Come Marching Home, 18, 19, 28, *29-36*, 46, 54, 60, 66, 90, 93, 104, 108, 114, 164 165, 166
Comfort Me With Apples, 20
The Days Between, 19, 22, 34, 45, 46, 49, 50, 52, 90, 102, 105, 110, 112, *113-22*, 134, 148, 153, 155, 156, 157, 161, 162, 163, 164, 165
Death Do Us Part, 17
Double Solitaire, 41, 46, 49, 52, 79, 85, 90, 102, 105, 108, 110, 114, 116, 128, *148-55*, 157, 159, 160, 161, 163, 164, 165, 166
Dream Dust, 17
Eden Rose, The, 16, 20, 28, 35, *36-45*, 46, 51, 52, 61, 62, 69, 75, 89, 102, 104, 108, 114, 116, 128, 129, 130, 150, 155, 160, 165
Footsteps of Doves, The, 41, 102, 110, *127-29*, 154, 165
Gate, The, 17
Girofle-Girofla, 15
Hour Town, 15
I Never Sang for My Father, 15, 16,

22, 23, 27, 35, 46, 60, 90, 93, 105, 114, 123, *134-41*, 149, 152, 156, 158, 163, 164, 166
I'll Be Home for Christmas, 34, 46, 49, 62, *129-32*, 161, 164
I'm Herbert, 17, 102, *132-34*, 157, 166
Love Among Friends, 137, 139
Love Revisited (*Lover Come Back to Me*), 21, 28, *45-53*, 60, 76, 102, 105, 108, 114, 117, 118, 127, 151, 164
"The Lunts Are the Lunts Are the Lunts", 124, 132
Midnight Dialogue, 17
Shock of Recognition, The, 48, *124-27*
Silent Night, Lonely Night, 21, 45, 46, 71, 78, 89, 90, 92, 102, *104-12*, 114, 115, 117, 120, 121, 130, 158, 159, 161, 164,. 165, 166
Sisters, The, 18
Solitaire, 46, *145-48*, 156
Solitaire/Double Solitaire, 22, 104, 119, 121, 125, *145-55*
Straw in the Wind, 18
Sublet, 20
Tailored Heart, The, 19
Tea and Sympathy, 18, 21, 22, 28, 46, 51, 54, 62, *69-81*, 89, 90, 96, 99, 102, 104, 105, 110, 112, 114-15, 118, 119, 120, 121, 123, 126, 129, 131, 134, 138, 145, 148, 154, 155, 159, 161, 163, 164, 165, 166
Undiscovered Country, 18
You Know I Can't Hear You When the Water's Running, 17, 22, 52, 123, *124-34*

WORKS—FILMSCRIPTS:
I Never Sang for My Father, 22, 101, *141-44*
Nun's Story, The, 21, 46, *90-93*, 98, 99, 119, 144, 146
Sand Pebbles, The, 22, 46, *97-101*, 138
Small Part of a Long Story, A, 22, *93-97*, 131, 164, 166
Tea and Sympathy, 21, *81-85*, 86, 87
Tiger, The, 93, 135
Until They Sail, 21, 46, *87-90*, 94, 104

WORKS—PROSE:
After, 18, 22, 25, 27, 46, 125, 141, 145, *155-62*, 165, 166
Birthright, 71, 96
Getting Up and Going Home, 167
"Katherine and Pity and Love and I", 71
The Necessity for Poetic Drama, 16
"No Final Curtain on the Ghosts of Grief", 21, 157
"Thoughts on Playwriting", 24

Anderson, Phyllis Stohl, 18-19, 21, 28, 86, 94, 106, 109, 111, 121, 156
Arrowsmith (Lewis), 20
Ashes (Rudkin), 94
Auden, W. H., 17
Auntie Mame (Lawrence and Lee), 112

Bach, Johan Sebastian, 132
Baker, George Pierce, 17
Balcony, The (Genet), 146
Barrie, James M., 17
Barry, Philip, 17, 18, 45
Basic Training of Pavlo Hummel, The (Rabe), 166
Battleship Potemkin (Eisenstein), 100
Becket, 141
Behrman, S. N., 17, 20, 53, 102
Best Man, The (Vidal), 102
Both Your Houses (Maxwell Anderson), 29
Boys in the Band, The (Crowley), 81
Brave New World (Huxley), 145
Brecht, Bertolt, 25
Brief Encounter (Lean), 84
Burning Bright (Steinbeck), 94
Burrows, Abe, 20

Cabinet of Dr. Caligari, The (Wiene), 84
Caligula (Camus), 115
Camille (Dumas), 18
Candida (Shaw), 69, 80
Candide (Voltaire), 30, 31
Caste (Robertson), 17
Cat on a Hot Tin Roof (Williams), 61, 72, 79, 97
Cates, Gilbert, 134, 144

Cavalcade of America, 20
Changing Room, The (Storey), 126
Chayefsky, Paddy, 19
Chekhov, Anton, 54, 67, 68, 69
Children's Hour, The (Hellman), 69, 81
Citizen Kane (Welles), 142
Clockwork Orange, A (Burgess), 148
Clurman, Harold, 20
Come Back, Little Sheba (Inge), 41, 62
Corbett, Leonora, 20
Coward, Noel, 17, 18, 45
Crucible, The (Miller), 72

Dance Me a Song (Wiman), 124
David Copperfield (Dickens), 20
Death of a Salesmen, (Miller), 34, 65, 137-38, 160, 163
deBeauvoir, Simone, 121
Delicate Balance, A (Albee), 155
Desire Under the Elms (O'Neill), 24
Doll's House, A (Ibsen), 127
Dooley, Dr. Tom, 22
Douglas, Melvyn, 141
Dramatists Guild, The, 23
Dream Girl (Rice), 20

End as a Man (Willingham), 69
Enemy of the People, An (Ibsen), 32, 35
Equus (Shaffer), 126

Family Way, The (Boulting Brothers), 94
Farenheit 451 (Bradbury), 148
Farewell to Arms, A (Hemingway), 20
Flanagan, Hallie, 28

Gassner, John, 19, 20
Ghosts (Ibsen), 33
Glass Menagerie, The (Williams), 88, 111, 135, 136, 137, 142
Great Gatsby, The (Fitzgerald), 138
Green Bay Tree, The (Shairp), 69

Hair, 125
Hairy Ape, The (O'Neill), 100
Harry and Tonto (Mazursky), 175n32
Hart, Moss, 20
Hedda Gabler (Ibsen), 88, 114
Hegel, Georg Wilhelm Friedrich, 39
Hellman, Lillian, 20
Hepburn, Audrey, 92-93
Herrick, Robert, 44
Hillyer, Robert, 17
Housman, A. E., 55
Howard, Sidney, 20, 102
Hulme, Kathryn, 90, 91

Ibsen, Henrik, 33, 34, 35, 36
Iceman Cometh, The (O'Neill), 160
Inge, William, 19, 27, 145, 165
Inherit the Wind (Lawrence and Lee), 112
Ionesco, Eugene, 132
Isherwood, Christopher, 17

James, Henry, 60

Kafka, Franz, 132
Kazan, Elia, 77, 112, 124, 154
Kerr, Deborah, 76

Lady L (Gary), 22
Last Meeting of the Knights of the White Magnolia, The (Jones), 113
Lawrence, D. H., 159
Lawrence, Jerome, 112
Lee, Robert E., 112
Lindsay, Howard, 20
Living and Dying (Lifton and Olson), 142
Long Day's Journey Into Night, (O'Neill), 16

McKenna, Richard, 98
Member of the Wedding, The (McCullers), 61, 141
Michener, James A., 87
Mielziner, Jo, 20, 65
Mill, John Stuart, 33, 35
Miller, Arthur, 20, 25, 27, 33, 124, 130
Minnelli, Vincente, 76
Mr. Smith Goes to Washington (Capra), 29

New Dramatists Committee, 20
"Night" (Pinter), 134
Night of the Iguana, The (Williams), 109

Night Thoreau Spent in Jail, The (Lawrence and Lee), 113
1984 (Orwell), 145
No Time for Comedy (Behrman), 53
Nun's Story, The (Hulme), 21, 106

Of Mice and Men (Steinbeck), 20
Oh! Calcutta!, 125
O'Hara, John, 117
On Death and Dying (Kubler-Ross), 156
O'Neill, Eugene, 17, 27, 100, 155
Osborne, John, 25
Our Town (Wilder), 114, 135
Out Cry (Williams), 25

Paris Bound (Barry), 38, 41
Petrified Forest, The (Sherwood), 20
Picnic (Inge), 169n15
Pillar of Society, A (Ibsen), 32
Pirandello, Luigi, 48, 134
Playwrights Producing Company, The, 20, 102-104
Private Lives (Coward), 41

Return to Paradise (Michener), 21, 87
Rice, Elmer, 102, 103, 113
Riders to the Sea (Synge), 89
Roman Holiday, 22
Romeo and Juliet (Shakespeare), 76
Roosevelt, Theodore, 138

Sandbox, The (Albee), 63
Sand Pebbles, The (McKenna), 22, 97
Sartre, Jean-Paul, 160
Seascape (Albee), 155
Sherwood, Robert, 17, 20, 102, 103
Skin of Our Teeth, The (Wilder), 114
Society (Robertson), 17
Spender, Stephen, 17, 157
Starlight Theater, 20
State of the Union, The (Lindsay and Crouse), 29
Sticks and Bones (Rabe), 166
Strange Interlude (O'Neill), 39
Streetcar Named Desire, A (Williams), 77, 116
Strindberg, August, 153, 159
Studio One, 20
Summer and Smoke (Williams), 20
Summertree (Cowen), 113
Swinburne, Algernon Charles, 70

Tarkington, Booth, 40
Texas Trilogy, A (Jones), 113
That Championship Season (Jason Miller), 74
Theater Guild, The, 22
Theater Guild of the Air, 20, 81
Theater of the Absurd, The, 132
Thoreau, Henry David, 72, 109
Trilby, 22

Uncle Vanya (Chekhov), 67

Valley Forge (Maxwell Anderson), 20
Van Druten, John, 17
View from the Bridge, A (Miller), 135

Whitehead, Roger, 112
Who's Afraid of Virginia Woolf (Albee), 63
Widow (Caine), 156
Wild Duck, The (Ibsen), 114
Wild Goose Chase (Warner), 148
Williams, Tennessee, 20, 27, 72, 77, 145, 166
Winslow Boy, The (Rattigan), 69
Wise, Robert, 97
Wordsworth, William, 51
Wreath and a Curse, A (Wetzel), 21, 54, *55-58*
Wright, Teresa, 22

Young Woodley (Van Druten), 69-70

Zweig, Stefan, 18